As it was in
the old days

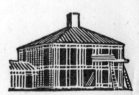

THE HOUSE

THAT

*by John
Gould*

JACOB

*William Morrow & Company
New York, 1947*

BUILT

fjl

DEDICATION

To my mother and father, first,
and to all the family who derive their beginnings
from the house that Jacob built. After that,
to such as helped us build the old house again—
Merle Brown as boss, and then Horace Hildreth, John
O'Connell, Mr. Fitzpatrick and Mr. Prout, Hubert A.
Bowie, Ross Cook and Mr. Gunderson, Joe Miller, Joe
Katula, Edward J. Dunn, Arthur Russell, Cleve and
Theo Bickford, George Coombs and Harry Edgecomb,
Wilbur Taylor, Brice Booker, Owen Gilman, Jess Goud,
Harry Reid, George Dugas, Gaulin & Goff, Adrien
Kinney, a man named Deland, Vance Harmon, Harry
Parady, John Brownell, Jr., Kenneth Harriman, Dennis
Polk, Fred Richard, Henry Morrison, Albert Dionne,
Fernande Lavoie, John Pelkey, Charles Miller and Earl
Pressy, Roland Leblanc, Richard Rines, Guy Morrill,
Mike Borcsak, George Gamrat, John Hric, Herbert Hun-
newell, Eugene Karkos, John Kushnir, John Ross, Leon
Leblond, Richard Poulin, Paige Rand, Stanley Parker,

Arthur Burt, Francis Soucie, Peter Sachin, Alwin Emerson and Sylvio Desjardins, Charles Cushman, Ralph Gould of Cape Elizabeth, Twaddle & Mitchell, Robert Hyde, Russell Stevens, John Janosco and Richard Kochis, Harry Wile and George Wile, Harold Littlefield, Douglas Brown, Mikey Woitko, Fred Rand and the Town of Lisbon for a cement mixer, John G. Hardy and Alexander G. Clapper, Ben and Ridie Wells, Jim Brown, and Dick and Polly Saunders, all well skilled in the arts and architecture. And Jacob Gould himself, who gave us a brick and a footscraper, and drew the designs on his trestle-board, and taught us that save the Lord build the house, they labor in vain that build it.

J. G.
Lisbon Falls, Maine
1947

‡6‡

ACKNOWLEDGMENTS

Portions of The House That Jacob Built *have appeared in* The Christian Science Monitor, The New York Times Magazine, Holiday *and* The Lisbon Enterprise *($2 the year postpaid).*

THE HOUSE THAT JACOB BUILT

OUR laddie was born in March, the night the house burned down. We have never felt this was an ideal combination. Around midnight my wife poked me and said it was time to take her to the hospital, so we headed out into a late spring snowstorm to become parents. We didn't waken Uncle Timothy, but we should have. Things went all right, and I was just starting back to the farm to wake him with the glad tidings when he came walking into the hospital with his nightshirt tucked into his pants.

"You're a new uncle!" I called at him, and he said, "We just lost our house."

About two o'clock somebody pounded outside his window with a board and got him out. The sheds and the back end of the house were already gone. These old Maine farmhouses go off like a box of matches when they start. Uncle tried to call us, but the fire had spread so he had time only to jump out the window. He grabbed all the clothes in one closet and heaved them out the window, grabbed a strongbox off his table with

‡11‡

some money and papers, and began to climb out on top of the clothes. Then he remembered the way people do during a fire, and turned to catch up two important treasures.

One was the Passenger Pigeon feather bed he slept on. Passenger Pigeons flew in clouds to darken the sun when this farm was first cleared, and we had this old feather-tick made from their breast plumage. Uncle Timothy never could sleep on anything else, and used to fluff it up every morning by himself. So he grabbed it off the bed and tossed it out on top of the clothes. Then he couldn't remember what the other treasure was, and he grabbed up instead an old Edison phonograph with a big horn on it and hove that out on top of the feather bed. With flames licking his Cal Coolidge nightshirt, he then jumped out on the phonograph and smashed it all to pieces.

That was all he saved.

He didn't worry about my wife and me when he saw the automobile was gone. I was parking it near the mailbox so we wouldn't get snowed in, and its absence meant just one thing. He got Mattie Mason to drive him down to the hospital, and we pooled our respective joys and sorrows. The fact is that Uncle Tim was so glad to have a new nephew he forgot all about the fire. The old farm needed a boy, he had reminded us ever since we came home married, and he worked almost every type of casual conversation around neatly to the subject of male progeny. We didn't dare to have a girl. Uncle had a boy's room all fixed up for him, with toys enough to last him ten years. He went around most of the time saving up things to tell the boy about.

So Uncle acted as if the loss of a set of buildings was the merest trifle in a lifetime of top-notch joy. It was graying off in the east when we got back to the farm, and the firemen were loading up their hose. A reporter from the Journal was there, and he asked about insurance and if we were going to rebuild.

"Give us two weeks," Uncle Timothy said, "and we'll have a roof over the baby's head."

It was more than two weeks, of course, and we had rather a miserable time of it for a while. But that was going on six years ago, and it doesn't look so bad from here. But we did lay up a log cabin in a very short time, without sparing the horses. A cabin is an easy and quick way to get walls up, and a couple of thousand feet of boards will go a long ways. It was a one-room affair, and was only a makeshift to bridge the gap between houses. The gap grew to five years.

Uncle Timothy left us during that time. He decided he needed a vacation, he said, and he packed all the new clothes he bought into a new suitcase we had given him, and he went off on a prolonged visit to all his nieces, nephews, cousins, and other relations we hadn't heard about. The lad grew to school age without the old fellow to guide him, and while it may have been just as well, it was too bad all the same.

It was about the middle of May when we had the cabin ready to live in, with probably as excellent a set of household properties as ever graced a log cabin. None of this back-to-nature business with us, we had class. Into the one-room cabin we crowded an electric refrigerator, washing machine, sewing machine, radio, vacuum, rotary ironer, and all the other conveniences we could stuff. We had the beds built overhead in one end, to allow use of the space beneath. For five years the thing we wanted next was always under something else.

The plans for our new home-to-be began to take

shape that summer, and we planned to start logging the next winter and get the boards stuck in the front field so the drying spring winds would season them. A year hence, barring the unforseen, we'd be in a house again. We sent out orders for plumbing, bought the windows, and then descended the clouds of war. It was five years before we stuck an ax in the second-growth pine of our far woodlot.

IF you put a Maine woman in a log cabin for five or six years, she gets delusions of grandeur—and the size of the house she wants taxes the whole township beyond all reason. It was so two hundred years ago when pioneer farmers got around to framing a dwelling. It was so in 1946 when World War II came to what was commonly considered an end. My great-grandfather built a house in 1780; I built one in 1946. It is, to all intents and purposes, the same house. I know what he went through.

Great-grandmother dwelt in a log cabin, a one-room affair laid up from old-growth pine. She had two children, and after a few seasons she began to promote something a little more suited to her needs. I can tell you just what she said, and just what he did. My wife had her log cabin and two children just like Great-grandmother. Then, just like Great-grandmother, she began to promote a dwelling more suited to her needs.

Washington Irving called such a house a "Yankee Farmer's Shingle Palace." Here in Maine we call them

"Woman Killers." You lay out about fourteen rooms on a sheet of builder's paper, and plan accordingly. In 1780 my Great-grandfather had untouched stands of virgin pine and spruce. In 1946 I had twenty-five acres of second-growth lumber almost as good as his. In 1780 he was burdened by the scarcity of pioneer days—he made his own bricks, nails, doors. He built the house with more sweat than wit. In 1946 I had all the lumber sawed and ready. But I also had a perverted kind of United States government to contend with—a government which no doubt had its supporters, but which had long ago forgotten the pioneer qualities that sired it, and which felt extremely little sentiment toward an old Jacob Gould of the Bowdoin Grant in the Androscoggin River Valley, and cared less that he once built the finest home in town. So I had to build my house with more wit than sweat, and began construction under the helpful regulation that no man can nail his own boards together unless he has complied with all political amenities in a book as thick as the butt log of a century-old oak.

Once, back before the fire destroyed it, I stood in the old house Great-grandfather built and admired his spirit, effort, accomplishment and success. Now, standing in the front hall of my own new home, I think I see the admiring shade of old Jacob bowing at me with respect, and lifting his hat in a gesture of submission. "Son," he is saying, "I was a piker."

He really wasn't, of course, but he probably would admire accomplishment himself, and it is true that his old "bee-hive" house, once burned, stands again on the old foundation, and his great-great-grandchildren are wiping their muddy bare feet on the same foot-scraper he once set in a block of granite by the back door.

Whatever pioneer lessons he gave to our beginnings have been renewed, symbolically, and the sun that once shone in his wide kitchen windows to warm a spot on the pine floor for the stub-tailed cat is again shining through wide windows, and another stub-tailed cat lies there asleep after lapping the froth from new-poured milk.

Dimensionally, the old house had certain measurements that the family could remember to the inch. We had two good photographs of it. It was nothing to draw the reproduction plans. But an old Maine farmhouse is not wholly a thing of dimensions, and carpenters can only build so far. When they finished we had a house. Some like it and some don't. But when we moved in we took with us certain effects the carpenters never thought about—we took with us the legends and traditions since 1780 and earlier, we moved in with a dose of make-believe that wasn't as far fetched as some might think.

Dimensionally, Great-grandfather built his house thirty-five feet square, this being the most economical shape for the maximum of interior floor and wall space. He added an ell that eventually reached out some seventy-five feet and ended in a rural convenience that was almost too far away to take seriously. Great-grandfather's house was predicated on the utility of a chamber vessel, and he had quantities of them at vantage points. Such utensils were not socially taboo then as they are now, and were not taken lightly as a subject of laughter. There was one old china combinet in the spare chamber that, taboo or not, was a favorite with all, and I wish we had it today.

What we do have today, of course, is a fine bathroom on the second floor, with a lesser one off the summer kitchen, and our ell is that much shorter. Our ell is really fifty feet long, with its cellar scientifically constructed as a vegetable and apple storage space. Under the house itself, still thirty-five feet square, we have a cemented basement that is much larger than we need. Great-grandfather's was never big enough on account of his chimney. The chimney he built was twelve feet square at the base, and gave him room for eight fireplace flues, including a double chimney for the big kitchen fireplace and the dutch oven. Each fireplace had its own flue, and by the time the chimney reached the rooftree it was cunningly brought together compactly. He burned the bricks himself, digging the clay from the brook just below us. One of his old bricks, saved when the house burned, is set into our new living room heato-later fireplace conforming to the tradition that something old should be built into each new home. It is a better brick than those we bought.

The inside of our home is modern. We have air conditioning, aluminum windows, indirect lighting, insulation, and all the other triumphs of construction. But when you drive up the hill past our lower orchard, the house you see is just like the one that burned. It has "six-over-six" windows, red paint, square central chimney, and the identical sunburst over the wide batten door. Great-grandfather, if he could walk up by the Northern Spy tree, would think sure it was his house. We like to think it is, too, and we aren't displeased with it because modern architecture belittles its lines.

Incidentally, the stub-tailed cat is a tradition. Uncle Timothy cussed cats with long tails because it took them so long to go through a door. In a Maine winter, we like a cat that gets in or out quick.

‡18‡

U NCLE Timothy never got to see the new house. He was no hand to write letters, but he got hopping mad if we didn't send him regular reports on the construction. His staying away from the old farm after the fire was sheer love, and his own idea. He felt he'd be in the way, and was more help absent. It did no good to write that we wanted him home.

He did have a hand in the work, even more than the dimensions he remembered for us. We built the house so Uncle Timothy would have his place in it. In time to come somebody may notice that the stairs are easy for an old body to climb. That the back stairway lets you out to do chores without waking everybody in the place. That the shop is laid out for puttering of the sort Uncle did, and that the furnace doesn't heat it. The shop has a ramdown stove, the kind Uncle Timothy would require. A stove you can spit in, he would have said. Not that he made too much of this freedom, but people do sometimes, and the principle is sturdy. A family with an Uncle Timothy wouldn't build a house he didn't agree with.

He was eighty-seven years old, and not a thing the matter with him. He said there wasn't, and so I know. A great many people in our family have died without ever having anything the matter with them. They get along in the prime of life, crowding ninety, and one morning they just don't wake up. Great-grandfather stayed until he was ninety-four, mostly because he was so busy he couldn't stop. He was hoeing corn one morning, and he came up to dinner saying the sun seemed to bother him more than common, and he thought he'd lie down and wait for the afternoon to cool a bit before he went back. His weary old body gratefully took repose on the kitchen couch, and all at once the family realized he was done with farming. It wasn't any great surprise, they simply became aware that the old man had slept off into the eternity awaiting him.

The passing of the old folks in a family like ours is always anticipated, particularly by the old folks. As a boy, it worried me to hear Grandfather tell about, "after I'm gone." He had no worries about it that I could see, he was just planning ahead so everything would be in good order when he got through. Our old folks had good lives, rich with their own doings—they lived seriously in their own sweat and by their own devices. It is good for a family to have old folks like that. Hardly any of ours ever had a last lingering illness. Most of them died on full stomachs. There was one old fellow, a half-brother to somebody away back, who ate six hard-boiled eggs just before he went to bed, and nobody felt the repast occasioned the demise. There was a lot of belief that "his time had come," as no doubt it had. It could be comforting that one's life was important enough to merit individual treatment in the celestial scoring.

Uncle Timothy was a lot like that. He was our last link with our ancient past, and having him at home with us was like having roots in the living water. It was our good luck that he was liberal, and didn't hang to the old things just because he got brought up that way. He was loyal to the old things that were good and abiding, but not hidebound. He was overjoyed when I drove home our first tractor, and he set out at once to sell the team. There was no remorse at the parting, save the crocodile tears he shed before prospective customers to show his grief at parting with such a fine pair. He did, though, keep a light horse to ride behind, and he detested automobiles. "Goes too fast," he'd say. "Makes you miss out on things to see. Nobody's in that much hurry."

He was never in a hurry. He couldn't stand people who were "right out straight," or "all heifered up." I never knew him to squabble with anybody, except for the legitimate differences arising from trade. "Life's too short." And he never played, as people think of playing. He took his enjoyment from doing things, and he liked all kinds of work. He used to say, "I hoe when I rest." The change of pace refreshed him, and he never felt the need of turning from work to take up some purely relaxing play.

The enjoyment he took from things he did was a kind of play, of course, and while he got it from the generations before, I'm glad we had him to pass the lessons along to us. Uncle Timothy's store of natural information was largely my source. I remember one spring he told of a partridge drumming, and a year later when I had forgotten about it he took me up in the woods to show me one in action. It is easily one of the finest sights in nature, and he had gone to hunt one up just for me. He showed me how to find a Bob-o-link nest. "The bird runs about ten feet before he flies up—look where he flies from, and then walk the circle and you'll find it. He first showed me a squirrel coming down a maple to drink from a sap spile, and showed how the squirrels sometimes chew a maple limb so they can have a sweet drink.

He read a lot, but didn't have any "taste." One thing was the same as another, except that he held fast what was good. He could talk about anything so folks would listen. His entire schooling was nine lovely months. He started when he was three; his sister was going, so why shouldn't he? He trotted behind her up to the Ridge School and stayed most of September. Then he stopped going until the next September, and every year after that he put in his Septembers attending school. At twelve he was accused of making advances at the teacher, which was just one of his stories, and was expelled. We know, however, that he learned more than some of the boys who got promoted, and after that he worked around the farm until he married Aunt Sarah.

Uncle Timothy never directed any of his talents in directions the great world applauds. His knowledge of human nature might have made him a great statesman. With his ability to dicker anybody could have been a great international banker. He was away ahead of his time in knowledge of farming, and the scientific agronomists who write books today merely make me think of Uncle Tim, who said the same things more understandably a generation ago. When I was a lad he harrowed in buckwheat and rye and explained it to the neighbors so he had most of them doing it.

‡ 2 2 ‡

Uncle Timothy needed children, but he never had any. Our boy was his life's biggest moment, and he had felt so sure of a boy that he started a bank account under the right name, "So's 't he can go to college." Even the college was a settled detail, because Great-grandfather had bought his land from Governor James Bowdoin, and you don't just up and ignore a connection like that.

After Aunt Sarah died—they always told me she was puny and ailing but the world's greatest stoic—Uncle Tim struck out and wandered around. He went most everywhere and tried a number of things. He made some money, but he said nobody knew how to bake beans and what with one thing and another he wanted to come home all the time. He'd stay around and then wander again, but after I got old enough to be company he came back for good.

After the fire he'd come back to visit us now and then for a few days, sleeping on a couch. The loss of the old home was a great hurt on his soul, and I think he felt he'd never live here again. He knew the dimensions of every room to the inch and figured how many stringers we'd need, and how long. He talked about coming back, but during those years things were too much in the future. He didn't get to know the lad too well, either—his visits were too infrequent and the boy was at that age. The last time he was home, the spring before we started building, he walked the lad up along by the pond and cut him a willow whistle. Uncle Timothy's eyes were red and swollen when he came back leading the lad by the hand. He said he blew so hard on the thing his eyes popped, but everybody knows there are tears to cutting a boy his first willow whistle and it's nothing to be ashamed of.

After the house started we wrote him every week—

long letters that named each board and counted all the nails. We drew sketches, and sent sticks with samples of paint on them. It was approaching home-coming time, and we had just sent a splotch of the red ochre and oil for the clapboards. The Shining Light Club had already held its shower and sent my wife home with a big basket of pretty things for the bathroom.

Uncle Timothy simply went to bed that night and never got up in the morning. They shipped him home to us, and the family gathered again in the little Free Will church and we went through the formalities. Perhaps there was a plan to it, and the older generations gave us only the stories and traditions to live with us in the new house. We don't even know which room would have been Uncle Tim's, because we were going to let him pick his own. He lies up under the maples and pines on top of the hill—a spot he chose for himself long ago, and one that I like myself as well as any.

MOST people Oh and Ah when they hear we built our house from lumber we cut on our own farm. What's wonderful about this, I don't know— it strikes me it is the best way to do it, and a lot of people are going houseless just because they didn't acquire a woodlot when we did. As far as I know the only lumber ever bought and brought onto this farm is whatever clapboards the place has needed. And I guess we didn't really buy them, because you can always swap pine boards for clapboards. But nobody around here has ever had a clapboard mill, and it was handier to buy them all made from away. We bought the clapboards on the new house back before the war when we were getting ready, and had them laid away in the barn before we started cutting timber.

The Eastern White Pine native with us is one of the nicest woods to work, but in late years it has taken a back seat to the lumbers from the west. It is legend here that in the colonial days the tallest of our pines were marked with the broad arrow of the King, whatever that meant, and were thus saved for masts for the Royal Navy. I imagine Great-grandfather didn't care much whether the King had a sail on his boats or not, and soon after he came up here he began whacking pines down as if they were weeds. He wanted fields to plow, and clearing land was hard work. To make it easier he burned most of the wood off, and in that way untold thousands of feet of beautiful board timber went up in smoke. Those old pines, which were called punkin pines, had aged a-standing until the wood was mellow and cheesy, and anybody who has ever whittled into a punkin to make a Halloween lantern will know why they were called punkin pines. It is no story that men could jump a yoke of oxen onto the stumps of those old trees, and turn them in a circle without their stepping off.

What they did was cut the trees down, and twitch the logs into piles. The piles were burned, the fires lasting for weeks, and after that they went along in the embers and poked seeds down with sticks. The pre-heated land was rich and crops were abundant. A few stumps had to be burned and pulled, and a year later they would plow. Burning a stump is quite a job, but can be done if you know how. Having a fire around it won't work —you have to build a fire on top, and then lay a pole across the blaze. Anybody with a fireplace knows that one stick will go out, but two will burn. So they kept a pole on top of the stump and this eventually burned a slot down into the ground, thus leaving the stump divided. It was easier to yank it out then.

Another trick of Great-grandfather's was to let the wind blow his trees down. He would cut nearly through a tree, but spare the exertion of going all the way. Then he would cut nearly through the next, and so on down the side of the hill. One day when the wind was right he would fell the first tree all the way, and it would start an avalanche. A good wind would sometimes take down the whole side hill, just as the first domino will tip over a whole row. It took a wind to do it right, but we always had plenty of wind.

Great-grandfather's logging took care of our original set of buildings and cleared what he needed for a farm. When Grandfather came along he cleared a couple more fields, and then specialized in cordwood until the old barn burned back after the Civil War. He had to get out lumber then for a new one, and he cleaned up all the old-growth stuff we had. Since that time we have been using what is known as second-growth—pine that runs from seventy-five to one hundred twenty-five years old, some a little older. It isn't as mellow a wood as the first-growth, but it runs fairly clear, and gives us what modern folks like best of all—knotty pine. In the old days carpenters around here would throw a board away if it had a knot in it, and some of the old time carpenters still turn their noses up a bit if you show them knotty wood. But since knots came into style our second-growth lumber has gone up in value, although I still like to work with clear wood and sell the knots.

When Grandfather was in his eighties, the last time he logged our woods, he didn't join in the work much because of his age, but he bossed the job and did his part by sharpening tools and seeing that the limb wood was cleaned up. He did drive the first load to the sawmill, and gave the whole village a thrill. He had picked up a pair of heavy horses for hauling the logs and was all set to take advantage of the first snow. The afternoon it started storming he rolled on ten or fifteen nice board logs and had everything ready for the morning. But during the night it rained, and by morning everything was a glare of ice. The wind shifted northerly and it turned cold at sun-up.

Grandfather would never put a team anywhere he wouldn't go himself, and as he never saw any place he wouldn't go, he soon had the horses hitched in and was on his way to mill with the first load.

The horses were fresh-calked; so they dug in gingerly as they started down off the Ridge, but shortly the load crowded them and they trotted a bit to keep ahead until they got down on level going. Grandfather, with the lines lengthened out to the last hole, sat on top the topmost log about seventeen feet in the air and snuggled inside his buffalo coat. The wind was bitter after the storm, but it was warm in where he was, and being as he was Grandfather and able to take his ease where he found it, he dropped off to sleep before he came to the village.

He was still asleep when he got there and remained asleep while he passed through it. The storekeepers were all out in the early morning chipping ice off their steps and putting salt on the sidewalks. They all had creepers on, and now and then a joyous shout would go up as this one or that one forgot himself for a minute and had to crawl indoors where he could find a purchase for standing up again.

At about this time Grandfather, unknowingly, had arrived at the slight down-grade that runs by the stores on Main street at the Falls, and the horses, feeling the coasting weight on their breechings, realized it was time to trot again or be run down. So they broke into a carefree canter and presently galloped by Fred Crosman's furniture store. Fred looked up and saw all the white pine logs in Maine sliding on the bias into his front window of dining-room pieces and crockery, and hid his face in his arms. But just then the tugs caught up and the team felt the collars tighten on their shoulders, and the load of logs was twitched back into line and off toward Roberts's.

Mr. Roberts, stabbing at ice on his stoop, retreated inside and suggested the clerks take to the rigging, after which he left the premises by a back window and waited for the building to collapse. But the tugs tightened again, and Grandfather snoozed on as the team straightened the load out and alternately threatened the shopkeepers the whole length of the street. They trotted on into the woolen mill yard without touching a thing, negotiated a sharp turn, and brought up at a walk on the bridge over the Androscoggin. The hollow noise of the bridge awakened Grandfather and he was pleased to find himself agreeably refreshed by his nap. He soon had the logs on the mill brow, and was dickering for a better saw price on account of the quantity of work he was to have done.

Some of the storekeepers, when I'm around, tell me about that morning even yet. They relate that they sat in their stores all day quaking with the thought of what missed them, and it was so slippery around town that nobody ventured in to trade all day.

There's a good story about Grandfather's logs, because he didn't get them sawed right away. He noticed the mill wasn't running that morning he came in, and then he found out they didn't have any saw. The man seemed reluctant to go into details, but the truth was he'd be shut down some little time for repairs, and Grandfather came home without finding out just why.

Well, the night before the storm, a big crowd had gone across the river to serenade a young couple that had been married. They don't do that much here now, but in the old days no wedding was over until the serenaders had come and gone and the happy couple had been privileged to feed them. This couple had a house over at Crosman's Corner, next the school, and the party formed at the Falls and walked over there to take place. It was a brisk winter evening with the fulling moon much in evidence, and they came to the foot of Kezarville Hill. This hill today is as much of a hill as it was then, although some of our roads have been widened and straightened to impress the tourists. The hill starts down by the river and twists back and forth on itself until it gets to the flat land above the river valley, and then the road runs straight to Crosman's Corner. The hill is maybe two hundred yards lengthwise, but it takes more time than that because of the curves, and it seems a mile when you walk up it.

Particularly on a winter night before the days of sanding the roads. Kezarville Hill was a glare of ice. The party struggled up, the boys helping the girls, and more than one slipped and fell. Horace Hodgdon had a worse time than anyone else, because he was carrying the big circular saw from the lumber mill. Everybody else had pans to beat and horns to blow and bells to ring, but Horace had brought the saw and a machinist's hammer. When the serenade started he anticipated a lot of fun. A circular saw has tonic qualities the jive orchestra business has neglected. When you whack one a good clip it will respond wonderfully, and people ten miles away will curse the day you were born. It will ring for weeks. In lumber camps they sometimes hang one up for a dinner gong, and when the cook pounds it with a long-handled blacksmith's maul it seldom causes any confusion among the lumberjacks as to whether or not they heard it. Horace is remembered around here as not being wholly bright, but this time he certainly had a gem of an idea, and he was correct in thinking this addition to the serenade would be worth the extra effort it took to bring it.

When it was time to go they all started back for the Falls with Horace on behind and the saw on a stick over his shoulder. Having served in the serenade, it must now be taken back to the mill for use on the morrow.

At the top of Kezarville Hill the party stopped and the girls tittered and waited for somebody else to start off on the slippery descent. Somebody said it was too bad they didn't have Davey Brackett's bob-sled and they could all ride down. This gave Horace an idea. He laid the saw down, sat on it, and hunched himself forward into a start.

The saw and Horace went about thirty feet in graceful and enjoyable style. Horace waved back gaily. The folks at the top of the hill cheered and laughed, and then the saw coasted around the corner and Horace was gone behind the firs by the roadside.

On the next turn he came into sight again, but he was going much faster and the saw was about ten feet off the ground. He turned the corner again and was gone, but when he came into sight again sometimes the saw was ahead and sometimes Horace was, and Horace was displeased either way and said so. The rest of the slide was in plain sight all the way, and although Horace ran on ahead for a short space the saw was under him when it hit a tree by the river bank and jangled most amazingly. The folks on the top of the hill slid and skidded down to bring whatever aid might be required. Horace's first words, when they arrived, were, "How moonly looks the moon!" and this has become an over-

‡31‡

worked catch-phrase around here, and is used today by folks who never heard of Horace. They picked him up saw and all and carried him home with everything still jangling and ringing at a fearful rate, and since that time nobody has ever slid down Kezarville Hill on a lumber-mill saw.

It was a good two weeks before the saw could be straightened, gummed, set and filed and hung on the arbor again for custom sawing, and Grandfather was vexed at the delay. About Horace, he said, "If he'd a-been bright it'd a-killed him."

DID you ever have a Maine farmer say to you, "I'd like to show you my cellar"? Once in a while some stranger to our ways feels this invitation couldn't possibly carry any special merit, and hastily makes excuses about having to catch a train, or being obliged to get to town before the stores close, and loses out in one of life's most golden opportunities. Never pass this invitation up, because seeing a cellar is worth all the time it takes.

What the farmer means, of course, is that he desires your opinion on the present condition of his cider barrel. The ancient traditions of the Yankee nature recoil spastically from the very thought of asking a man to take a drink. Come to think of it, I have never had a neighbor of mine address such an invitation to me. By indirection he directs your attention, and under no pretext are you to acknowledge openly that the cider has any esoteric qualities. Your job, as one invited to inspect a cellar, is merely to see if the cider measures up to the customary average of the vicinity, and to inform the farmer in direct terms just how you think it is coming along, and whether or not it stands a chance of being good vinegar at some future date which should be estimated with care.

Cider is sometimes employed to excess, but most Maine farmers regard it casually, with no particular thought to its intoxicating possibilities. Cider, considered clinically, is an alcoholic beverage of mighty propensities and has been known to Maine folks since the first apple tree flowered and set fruit on these shores. Its flavor is usually more pleasant, if considered objectively, than any of the commercial beverages advertised so expensively. For those who are looking for a quick, positive, irrevocable drunken stupor, it cannot be equalled among all the fruit juices or distillations. Too much cider is bad business, and a lumberjack who takes the jug into his bunk is regarded as hibernating and is struck off the payroll until spring. Yet Maine cider is not a commercial commodity, and as far as I know cannot be purchased in package stores. It has never been elevated much above the cellar status.

Perhaps the reason is that Maine farmers accept the processes of nature, and look upon cider only as a way-station in the chemical change of sugar liquid. If you want vinegar you have to have cider first. And the better the cider the stronger the vinegar. The interesting meantime, when acetification is yet to come, deserves careful and considered investigation, but only in a scientific spirit and with due regard for the social obligations of an upright citizen.

In our old house, the cider barrel was so esteemed, and although all of us from Great-Aunt Susan down have had some business with it off and on, ours was never a drinking family, and nobody ever drank cider

‡34‡

without afterward commenting dutifully on the likelihood some day of its making a sharp vinegar and excellent pickles.

Grandfather knew how to make cider, and if you pay attention I'll tell you his secret. He had a barrel pressed, and with it a five-gallon carboy extra. He brought them home, and by rigging a plank could get the barrel into the cellar alone. The barrel was horsed up with the bung at the top, and then he drew the plug and left the bung open. At this point the cider was freshly pressed and was delicious beyond description. Everybody had as much as he wanted, and some of us more than we needed.

Since sugar is the basis of acetic acid, the sweet apples from the front-yard tree made the best cider—a rich honey-thick syrupy cider with a dark-brown color. After the barrel was horsed up we children used to go out in the barn and get some oat straws, which we stuck through the bung, sometimes four heads together sucking carefully because the straws were delicate. When we had enough we'd stick the straws up over a beam for next time. For two or three days we had the most wonderful beverage, and then we noticed the cider would begin to suck back. It smarted our tongues, and there would be a froth around the bung. It was "working."

It really did work; it shoved all the chum in the cider, the little smidgins of apple that had come through the press-cloth, up through the bung and out in the froth. Grandfather patiently filled the barrel from the carboy everytime he went by, to compensate for what we children sucked out and what worked out, and this kept on until one day the cider stopped working altogether and there was no more froth. We children had long since stopped sucking at it. By this time the cider

‡ 3 5 ‡

was about ready to leap out and snap at us, and as far as we cared it had no future at all.

But Grandfather knew better. Now it was ready to ripen. He drove in the bung tight and went off about his business. Time elapsed, and one day or one evening he would have occasion to say, "I'd like to show you my cellar." Folks who went down with him may or may not have noticed the preserves, the butter and eggs salted down, the pollock hanging up and the salt pork in the barrel. They may or may not have observed the potatoes, beets, carrots, turnips, or the apples. But away over in the corner they did discern a barrel with a spigot in it, and a glass or a dipper upside down on the top.

Twice that I know about Grandfather's matter-of-fact cider barrel achieved proportions the temperance movement might resent. Once was on a hot summer day when Grandfather took a load of tomatoes to Lewiston, and left two hired men mowing out the front-field swale with hand-scythes. These two worthies mowed for a time, and then commented mutually on the desirability of refreshment. This led to speculation on whether or not Grandfather had some cider. The speculation caused wonderment, and the wonderment resulted in investigation. The afternoon was magnificent. They would mow a swath, and then repair to the cellar and taste the cider. They undoubtedly observed an improvement each time they returned, for each time they lingered longer and tasted more.

In the end they were beyond physical pain, and were able to arrange a fight between them. At this point Grandfather returned home, having sold his tomatoes for a good price, and he found the two hired men down in the swale calling each other perfectly awful names, and trying to hook their scythes over each other's necks.

Grandfather discharged them, but not until he had watched the fight for a time. He sat down under a tree and admired the spectacle, and felt he might never again have the chance to watch men fight with hand-scythes and he didn't want to nip opportunity in the bud. They didn't hurt each other, and Grandfather figured they were so far gone they weren't likely to. He found out the next day they'd left the spigot running, and his barrel of cider was gone forever and the cellar smelled liquorish.

The other time was on a cold winter night, when Sam Bellamy dropped in to get warm on his way past in the sleigh, and Grandfather thought to induce a tincture of rosiness by fixing up some mulled cider. I understand mulling implies certain arrangements in some imbibing circles, but to us folks up here mulled cider is nothing but a glass of cider with a red hot poker stuck in it. Again, the drink has no connection with fellowship, conviviality, or boozing. It was more of a tonic, a pleasant diversion not to be taken unless one had definite need for it. Being chilled to the bone constituted as much need as anybody could think of, so Grandfather stuck the poker between the two thick beech sticks in the cookstove, and went down cellar with the brown pitcher. He mulled Sam a good one, and Sam said it made him feel better. Sam said he didn't mind if he did, so Grandfather mulled him another, and Sam said he hadn't seen such magnificent cider in many a day and he certainly would like to take some of it home to lay away against another time.

Grandfather was flattered by this display of good judgment over his vinegar probabilities, and he went down and drew off a jug for Sam to carry along with him. It was the wrong thing to do; Sam didn't carry it home—he began to dally with it as soon as he was out of sight, and didn't even wait to mull it. The snowstorm shut down harder as Sam left, and it was a blinding blizzard by the time he got halfway to Higgin's Corner. Sam must have counted on the old horse, but the old horse failed him. The horse went off the road in belly-deep snow, stuck his head in under the limb of a pine, and stood there to wait out the storm. Sam didn't know the difference, and he finished off the jug sitting right there. They found him the next day, frozen to death with the thumb of his mitten looped through the jug handle.

Grandfather never really got over this matter, and never again in his lifetime did he invite anybody down to see his cellar, or bring up a dipper of cider to mull. His cider pressing from then on was strictly a vinegar proposition, and the barrel was never fitted with a spigot until the contents would cut your throat in a great jagged wound.

The cellar under the old house went around the big chimney base, and had nothing in the way of a furnace in it. Central heating was unknown back then, but it wouldn't have worked anyway, because you can't keep garden produce in a heated room. The floor was hard-packed dirt, on the clay, and it was almost a bit skiddy. Walking on it with bare feet leaves you remembering the clammy feeling forever. In my time the cellar was barely five feet deep, but they say back when the house was built Great-grandfather had left at least seven good feet between the dirt and the joists. You see, every turnip that came in brought some of the garden with it, and countless turnips, potatoes, carrots and beets had brought in whole cartloads of dirt in time, and each year the floor built up that much.

Our cellar had a well in it, which is not common. Grandfather had torn out part of the old wall once, and had laid up a new one under the house. Frost had heaved Great-grandfather's stones out of line. When he finished this job he had the cellar full of rocks, and he began carrying them out one at a time. A tramp came along as tramps did in those days, and asked for food and lodging, and work. Grandfather told him to dig a well in the cellar. It was really Grandfather's idea to have a hole dug and bury the rocks. But they found a good vein of water, and they finally used the rocks to stone up the well. Then they brought in a big flat rock for a cap, and the pump in the sink overhead dated from then on. Before that water was carried in pails from the barn.

That well was the last resting place of the ramrod from Grandfather's Civil War musket. I have the musket, and it was not lost in the fire. It happened to be at an aunt's, because they had used it in a store window display. Long ago when the pump in the kitchen sink used to catch when the winter nights were too cold for the range, they would take the ramrod from the musket, heat it at the fire, and poke it down in the barrel of the pump. It would sizzle, a jet of steam would fly up, and after two or three heatings the ramrod would chunk down through the ice, and they would get water again. But one day an uncle, who was then a small boy, let go the end of the ramrod just as it chunked down through, and the ramrod went in the well. It was never recovered, although I wish I had it. I've got another ramrod now, but it isn't the one Grandfather brought home with him from the wars.

I think the bees and the cream ought to round out the story of that old cellar. The cream was set on the cellar floor to sour for butter. This, today, is strictly against all health laws, and a man may be fined and maybe shot for selling sour cream such as our ancestors ate and lived on to be ninety and better. It was not cold on the cellar floor winter or summer, but was cool. It was the right coolness for the proper activity of the milk bacteria, and they went to work with a will and made that thick, sour cream that milk companies condemn as an instrument of filth. Louis Pasteur was probably a boon, but he has prevented a lot of people from knowing about the lovely things lactic acid bacteria do to a pan of rich Jersey milk that is left the right time on the damp floor of an old Maine cellar. I will not speak of it further, as this would irritate former residents who have almost forgotten this luxury, but I will confide that nobody had a better cellar for it than we did.

The bees were Grandfather's idea, and it was a good one. It is hard to winter bees in this climate, and most beekeepers go to the bother of special covers, lined with shavings and tar-paper. Some pile up straw and even level dirt over the backs of the hives. Some men build special houses, airtight, where the bees may be warm. Bees do not freeze up in the winter, the way ants do, but stay alive through the coldest weather. They eat their honey, and this generates heat, and when the weather is forty below the center of the hive is almost at summer heat. If the hive's stores are depleted, the bees freeze, which is really a case of starvation and not of freezing. The colder the weather, the more honey it takes to put them through. So Grandfather figured his cellar was all the shelter bees ought to need, and every fall he carried them down hive by hive and stuck them under the apple bins. Thus they sometimes came out on such occasions as the January thaw, and when extra rambunctious would seize upon any excuse to brad the hired girl who went down for some plum preserves, Grandmother who went down to select baking potatoes, or even Grandfather who went down to inspect the cellar. Grandfather insisted that bees had stung him so much they didn't hurt any more, but everybody else lamented this inference that anybody should just let a bee sting to reap the benefits of immunity in later years. Grandmother in particular had many words that she used in this connection.

The old cellar, of course, is gone. The ashes were cleaned out after the fire, and we hired a caterpillar bulldozer to come in and excavate a new and bigger area. We capped the old well with concrete, and sunk a copper tube in it. We pushed Great-grandfather's walls away and poured cement. We put in a furnace with forced hot air, and sealed off the part we plan to keep vegetables and apples in. It isn't much like the old cellar, but times change. I would like to show it to you sometime.

IT is going to be interesting to see how long it takes our new house to accumulate a collection of Yankee odds and ends after the manner of the old-timers. Right now the pine-clean shed attic is empty. And an empty shed attic in Maine is the most ridiculous thing in the world.

The shed attic of the house that burned was a treasure chest, and even the most neat and orderly had to admit the collection had a value if the owners could stand having it around. Just what that value was is problematical, and depends on daily needs and also on the passage of time. "Keep a thing seven years," the saying goes, "and you'll find a use for it." This being so, it has been easy for down-easters to keep things twice seven years, and everybody knows that time alone is the factor that will bring around a use.

My father once kept a ski seventeen years. We used to make fun of him about it, but he never admitted any likelihood that he was wasting the space it took up. It was stuck over a beam in the barn, and it probably dated from my first pair of skiis. It probably happened that I broke the ski instead of my neck, and came home carrying the surviving ski just as if somebody could do something with it. Probably inherent thrift prompted me to carry it home, and probably if the lad brought home one ski today I would still keep it. But my father did keep it—he stuck it over the beam, and we youngsters grew up and it was still there. It was there seventeen years before my father took it down one day and cut three feet off one end to make a dandy paddle for stirring the pig's barrel. The trouble with us who laughed, of course, was that we thought a ski had to be used for skiing. Father, with centuries of retained oddities behind him, had no such illusions, and when he wanted a pig's paddle he took down his ski and made one. An interesting treatise, no doubt, could be made about the adaptations involved in the making of pig's paddles, and the truth probably is that no State o'Mainer ever went out and got a new, clean board for such a tool.

Grandfather once, somehow, picked up a roller skate, and he kept that for a long time, too. It was over the barn door on a shelf for long years, and he frequently commented that he was keeping it for some one-legged man who wanted to roller skate. Then one day he got it down and put it under the wheel of a cart and slid the cart sidewise back under the barn, and a whole new era of usefulness was opened. We used that roller skate for everything—moving stoves, barrels, anything heavy that needed to be slid around. It handled such big loads it sagged in the middle, and we had to lay it on the anvil and pound it straight again.

There was no limit to the cultch up in the old shed attic. Grandfather was an auction addict, and usually went in a hayrack. He'd drive the hayrack into the yard just beyond the fringe of the crowd, and would perch there on the rail listening to the sale. He didn't bid always, unless he saw something he needed or could turn to profit, but he always bought. It was supposed to be quite a joke in these parts, and probably a lot of people thought Grandfather was queer about it.

Auctioneers are actors too, and they know when to pull some comic show to put new life in a crowd. When the bidding dulls off a country gathering always likes the old thunder-jug routine. Judge Cummings, who was our auctioneer around here in those days, always judged the over-all success of a sale by the number of chamber vessels he found in the list. When he noticed people were talking in the back crowd, and folks were wandering off to sit down and rest, he'd whip out one of these items and wave it aloft with folksy abandon. He'd shout, "How much am I bid for this rare old Ming vawse?" The crowd would come to life, all manner of hearty comments were passed up, and Judge Cummings would respond. After he had rejuvenated the audience, it was necessary to find somebody who would buy it.

Over a period of years it became the custom for Grandfather to buy it. Grandfather never bid on one in his life, and as far as I know never used one until he was old. But there he sat on the rail of his hayrack, above everybody else, his whiskers an identifying mark to all, and sometimes he was even asleep there in the sun. "Sold to Tom Gould for ten cents!" Judge Cummings would bark, and the crowd would roar. The hilarity accumulated as time went by, and Grandfather would come home with one more item for his "ceramic collection." He referred to it that way, and auction crowds knew that Judge Cummings had sold him scores of them.

‡44‡

As far as the mugs went, Grandfather didn't lose any money. He used them for watering the hens, picked garden stuff in them, and acted as if he never knew they were supposed to have a more private purpose. One rose covered china mug was kept behind the stove for the dog to drink out of, and our family never thought anything of it. It made a wonderful dish for that, and if the dog didn't care, why should anybody else? Many times visitors to the house had a surprise when they looked over to see what that slupping noise was, and saw what the dog was doing.

Grandfather bought other things at auctions, though. He did it much the same way. He'd sit there paying little attention, and the old Judge would put up a bucket with no bale on it, a cracked water pitcher, and a box of tin knives. Nobody would want such a treasure, and nobody would bid. So the Judge would add a keg of reclaimed, mixed nails, a set of shoemaker's tools, and a box of empty patent medicine bottles. Then he would ask for bids again, and nobody would bite. So he would add a pickle crock with no cover, a box of mowing machine rivets, a wire dressmaking form, and a 'coonskin cap. Still nobody would bid. Every auction has junk like that to be worked off, and the trick is to get rid of unwanted stuff by selling it along with one item of sound value. The problem was to locate the sound item without venturing too great an attraction. So Judge Cummings would add still more junk until finally he was surrounded on the platform with odds and ends that nobody would take as a gift. To extricate himself he would finally yell, "Sold to Tom Gould for ten cents!" Grandfather would get down off his rack, haul out his wallet, extract a dime, claim his goods, and pile them in the hayrack.

I wouldn't say that our shed attic was the recipient of all these rarities. But in time a good many potential relics went up the steep back stairs and were piled under the eaves. Not only that, but as our family went on living in the house our own cast-offs were added. In time people forgot which were ours and which came home in the hayrack. The shed attic was the place for accumulations, and whenever you wanted anything you went up there and got it.

Probably the hardest thing to explain about this accumulation business is the fact that we *did* go up there and get things. The junk was useful, and all it needed was time. I remember once a sheet of tin on a planter corroded out, and there was no time to send away for a replacement. We got an old washboard from the shed, ripped off the tin, pounded it flat on the anvil, cut it, and fixed the planter. One time we took a roller off an old wringer, fitted it on the hay door of the barn, and had a raceway for the trackfork rope—this saved wearing the rope and the sill. And I was partner in this sort of thing for relatively few years—it had been going on two generations before I knew about it.

The junk in the shed attic should not be confused with the junk in the wagon shed attic. Up over the wagon shed Grandfather kept his old iron. That was why the twelve by twelve beams bowed down a couple of feet or so. An inventory was impossible. Some of it were known items like ox-cart tires, mowing machine shoes, pump handles, scraps of logging chains, rocker plates, or maybe sled irons. But some of it was just old iron—bent bolts, assorted nuts, hinges, broken pieces of old farm machinery. Your guess is as good as anybody's. It was laid by, piece by piece, against possible use in some busy day when there wasn't time to fix things right. Many a time folks on a farm need a piece of strap iron with bolt holes six inches apart. Or maybe seven inches. You never know. It depends on what breaks. Grandfather would go up and stir around in this pile and come down, usually, with just the thing.

Since the fire I've missed that scrap iron more than a little, and have made many a trip to town that would have been unnecessary if I just had an accumulation of cultch to stir around in. It is true that my machinery and equipment is in better condition for it, because when I want a certain size of bolt I go buy it. Grandfather simply dug out the nearest thing he could find to the right size, and then spaced out with washers until he could take up the nut. He had plenty of washers, because when the fixed implement at last broke down all the way, he salvaged things like that and carried them back upstairs. It was a self-perpetuating kind of fortune, and you never caught up with it.

Of course the fire cleaned all this stuff out. The iron was red hot for two days, and then we piled it on a cart and hauled it to the dump. From that time on this farm has got along without keeping so many things, although I have made a start and can show you a good assortment of horserake teeth, bent nails, and a few pieces of broken chain. None of these is in the new house yet, and in spite of my firm belief in the wisdom of laid-away treasure, I don't intend to take them in. But the old house was new once, too, and I imagine Great-grandmother resolved to keep the shed attic clean in her day. Auctions aren't the same as they used to be, and we'll probably be spared the bringing home of unsalable items. Well, time will tell, and if the collection gets a good start in my time, it's nice to know I double-timbered the floor of the shed attic.

A SINK and a kitchen range were the biggest problems we had connected with building a house. In this modern day and age neither is manufactured with a Maine farm house in mind, and the things they try to sell you are a disgrace to any well-intentioned woman who plans to cook anything and then wash the dishes afterward. I gather the fault lies largely with the way our enlightened government conducted matters during World War II. Those in charge of keeping production unproductive had the notion everybody does, or ought to, live in an apartment. The things that came along for new houses were all about that size. Furnaces were mostly in little sizes for small homes. And, of course, as with everything else that is done on a national scale, the peculiarities of Maine were ignored. The idea of anybody in Maine buying a small furnace is an absurdity exceeded only by the fact that nobody was permitted to make any big ones.

So we started out looking for a real farm sink and all we could find anywhere were the mass-production prefabricated-house kind that will handle three teacups and a nappy at a time. The salesmen would all say, "The trend is toward a small sink." Then they would show us some pastel shades, and it was on such a hunt we first heard about garbage grinders. My wife was much upset by that. "The very idea!" she said. The salesman thought it was wonderful, and pointed out a house no longer had to have nasty old garbage hanging around until a man comes to get it.

Garbage, as a term, is non-existent around here. We call it swill and we take it down to the hens or the pigs every time anybody goes to the barn. The hens and pigs are glad to get it. It never accumulates beyond what we have left over from each meal. The idea of grinding it up and washing it down a drain is enough to make any proper farmer gnash his teeth.

It wasn't too long ago that Grandfather kept even the dishwater and used it in the hog's victuals, and it isn't so unsound a thrift as it appears. They used a great deal of salt pork and fat meats in those days, and after each meal Grandmother rinsed the plates off with boiling hot water. This flushed off the grease, and the water from it was dumped into the barrel in the barn where Grandfather stirred up his hog slops. Anything that would entice a hog into extending himself went into the barrel, including a certain amount of meal and middlings. Grandfather claimed the fat from the dishwater would put weight on a hog whether he got any corn meal or not. All the skimmed milk went into the barrel, too, and by the time the hog got it the concoction was ripened to his taste. It isn't everybody knows how to feed a hog, and it is still true that you can't afford to raise one if you have to buy grain for him. Dishwater, boiled turnips, old potatoes and whatever are what makes profit on a hog. And no matter how convenient a garbage grinder may be, we didn't think it just suited a kitchen sink on this particular farm.

The kitchen sink is a mighty serious part of a country kitchen. How serious is best explained by the old story about the farmer who, at bedtime, started for the kitchen and turned to ask his wife, "Did you wipe down the sink?" She said, "Yes," and he said, "Well, I did want a drink of water, but I'll wait till morning." Wiping down the iron sink was the last thing the farm wife did before she came into the other room. Sometimes these sinks had no drainpipe to them, and were known as dry sinks. All the water had to be carried outdoors and dumped. Any that spilled into the sink had to be sopped up with a sink cloth. Why they bothered to have a sink at all is something to wonder about, but the women were glad to have even a dry sink. As time went along and they got hand pumps, and then sink spouts, life must have seemed wonderful.

Even the sink spout has overtones that endear it to farm people. They whistle. What they whistle depends on which way your kitchen faces, but as most Maine homes keep the kitchen toward the south, and that is where our nasty weather comes from, it is usually a southerly wind or storm that makes the sink spout whistle best. The farm woman knows the minute the wind swings southerly, and if her husband says he thinks we're in for a rain, she can confirm his suspicions by saying the sink spout has been whistling. A spout connected with a septic tank can't whistle, of course—it's only those that stick straight out from the side of the house and have two boards nailed together for an extension. You'll always find the hens out around the drain. When the

‡50‡

spout whistles you can look out and see the south wind blowing back their tail feathers.

Wet, dry or otherwise a farm sink wants to be big. Sink makers don't seem to know what farm women do in their sinks. These big houses we have up here aren't eight-hour wonders poured from a tank truck. Building a farm home is more than a "housing" matter. This is a business, here, a kind of a factory, with production problems and people coming in hungry. Most of the sinks we saw in the stores were hardly bigger than the pan my wife makes Johnny-cake in, and that pan isn't any too big at that. The sink we had in mind would be big enough to dump a crate of strawberries in while we wash them for freezing.

It might, at the same time, also hold the dishes from dinner in the other end, and leave room to clean a mess of trout in the middle. If things go along here on schedule, it wants to be a sink the children can swing a waterwheel in, and sail a few boats. Something you can run a decent tide in. Nobody in all the world knows, but us, what we might do in a sink. We certainly aren't interested in buying a sink whose dimensions include drainboards. We heard of a sink one day that was long enough to suit us, and when we saw it the thing had drainboards attached, and the sink itself was about the size of a bread pan.

It also had a cabinet with it—all one piece. We went back the next week and showed the salesman that our thirty-quart kettle wouldn't fit in the cabinet. He said, "But people don't use kettles like that today." We do. We make soap in it, and boil off the maple sugar, and it isn't a bit too big for a boiled dinner. We suppose people who live in apartments don't eat boiled dinners. Or lamb stews. You ought to see the dumplings push up over the top of that kettle when we make a lamb stew. And this kettle has to go under the sink. That's the way it was in the old house.

Anyway, we had quite a time finding just the sink we wanted, and ultimately got one by going to the hotel and restaurant people. We found you can have a sink any size you want if you just tell these people what suits you. Nothing would suit us unless you can wash all the milk dishes in it, including the churn and butter molds. What we wanted, of course, was a good old-fashioned sink we could live in.

As to the stove, we found disaster has struck there, too. The old stove founders in Bangor, who supplied the curious needs of chilly Maine for so many years, had gone out of business and had sold their patterns to a Portland concern who were now making pretty all-white ranges. Our new house has an all-white range in it, but it is a wood-burning range.

Ranges nowadays run to gas, coal, oil and electricity —four fuels not produced on our farm. They are nice to use and a lot of Maine farmers have turned to them. I look at it this way—we have more wood in our back land than we would ever use up if we kept a perpetual fire going. It costs us absolutely nothing beyond the labor of getting it. The labor of getting it is good for me, it gives me plenty of healthy exercise in the open, and I have a power saw for working it up.

I also have a wife who has learned that good hard wood is the best fire for cooking. She admits this readily, at the same time agreeing that other fuels may make less dirt, may be easier to handle, and may suit the novice. But she knows how to put that last brown on a pan of biscuits by sticking the right amount of dry alder in at the last minute, or how to keep the beans going all day Saturday so they have that wood-cooked supper-time complexion. Folks who tell us beans can be baked with oil, gas, coal or electricity are addressing the wrong audience.

The stove we had in mind ought, naturally, to be one like that Aunt Martha bought for the old kitchen. Great-grandfather didn't believe in stoves, and she did all her cooking on a hearth until he died. But when he was gone she hot-footed it to the city and bought a stove. It was worth all she paid to cook on, and worth a thousand dollars more just to look at. Big as it was—with nickel all up and down and shelves and warming ovens and hot water tank—it fitted right into the old fireplace so not more than a third of it was out in the room. The hottest place in the world was behind that stove, and in the winter the only warm place on the farm was within a few feet of it. I can remember how Grandmother Rebecca would be heating it up to brown biscuits, and Chump, the dog, would have to crawl out from under it with his tongue hanging down. Anything that would make Chump move had power and force.

Anyway, we went on a hunt for an honest old Maine cook-stove, having in mind something like Aunt Martha's with a firebox that opens on the side. A side opening is a great idea, arrived at with simple Yankee discernment, and allows the wife to instigate more heat without lifting the kettles off the front covers.

They tell about the old woman over beyond here who had a stove like that, and her husband exploited the possession shamefully. He would sit on a chair and whittle while she fed gray-birch sticks in at the side. Gray birch is not a good wood, and gets burned only because it is prolific and easy to cut. The trees seldom get very big, so the farmer usually cuts them "sled lengths" and brings them to the house anywhere from eight to fifteen feet long. So this old fellow made his wife burn sled-length sticks in her stove. As fast as they burned off at the end, she would run them in another length, resting the butt on a chair off across the kitchen. This woman is said to have remarked that Hell would suit her fine, as she would like to help Satan stoke his fires with something better than gray birch.

The stove in the old house was such a stove, its black black and its nickel bright. Grandmother kept rags of this and that on one of the shelves to swab it after each meal, sometimes with fat, sometimes with vinegar, sometimes with patent purchases. The stove was an integral part of the family, requiring attention regularly. And it rewarded such attention. It seemed smart to get one like it and keep right on.

But we couldn't get one. The makers had failed in their obligation to the state, and gone out of business. You couldn't even get one of those four-cover jobs so long a favorite in the woods. The kind with an oven door on both sides—they say you can pass biscuits through it once and they are done. They are absolutely the best baking stove ever invented and have persisted in lumber and sporting camps because they are not high enough for a kitchen. Women have to keep their work up where they can be chummy with it. A man in camp wants his stove down where he can put his feet on the hearth, and can reach over and dump his pipe without standing up. This was the kind of a stove that Bangor firm made for Ed Grant, the way I heard it. He wrote down from Kennebago and said he was tired of stoves he had to blow in to get them going, and couldn't they for heaven's sake or some words to that effect make him a stove that would burn with a good brisk draft?

So they made this stove, and Ed took it in to Beaver Pond in the winter on a sled, and set it up. He lit it, and then went down to the pond to chop a hole and get some water, and when he looked up the stove pipe was sticking up out of the top of the camp about fifteen feet. He rushed back and found the stove right up against the roof. The draft was so brisk it had picked the stove right up off the floor. Ed always said he was proud of what he did. Most men would have reached up and shut the damper, and let the stove drop back on the floor with a bang and smash. But with presence of mind he turned the damper a little bit at a time, and eased the stove back onto the floor.

This stove was the same kind the professors from Massachusetts Institute of Technology saw up at Kokadjo, and admired the untutored guide who had set it up. The guide had it about four feet off the floor on chunks of yellow birch, and the professors noticed it and observed how well it heated the room from that point. They computed the floor area and the cubic contents of the camp, and figured the B.T.U. output of the stove was increased tremendously by this position. They wondered how an uneducated woodsman could figure a thing like that out, and they marveled at native intuition. They complimented him on his rule-of-thumb arrival at an ingenious engineering conclusion. He said he put the stove up that way because he didn't have enough pipe to let it sit on the floor.

Anyway, the old line of real Maine stoves had been discontinued. We hunted up the people in Portland who had the pattern, and they said they were making the same identical Atlantic Range our grandmother used, except that it now had a white front. The inside hadn't been changed a bit. It burned wood. It had all modern improvements, such as a top that wouldn't turn white, and insulated sides. It also had a new kind of clean-out, and the man grinned at us and said we mustn't be fooled by the little time clock and the salt and pepper shakers on top. The streamlining, he said, was out of deference to people who wanted stoves like the women use in the cities, but an old Atlantic customer would find the cooking parts of the stove the same as had so often roasted great Thanksgiving dinners all up and down the state. He said we couldn't go wrong with an Atlantic, no matter how it was dressed up. So we bought an Atlantic.

It is a gorgeous stove, and the biscuits that come from it make just as fine a supper as any Grandmother ever baked. The white front fools people who come in, and at first they think we have electricity or bottled gas. Some even think we have oil, and sniff, as every kitchen that burns oil has a smell. But it is still a wood burner, and I bring down my wood every winter just as before. And like all the little boys who have grown up on this old place, our lad has the sad but useful obligation of keeping the woodbox filled. Like the rest of us, he will grow up to look upon women as wasters of wood, but makers of nice things to eat.

CERTAIN edifices, usually of a sacred nature, are destined never to be completed—workmen toil on and on through untold generations until the human race itself is exhausted, but the building is still a-building and nobody ever really intended to finish it. I do not understand this method of tackling a job, because with our own farmhouses in Maine it was possible to have the same indefinite attitude toward a finished product, and yet with straightforward Yankee practicality the work was terminated. The house was never finished, which satisfies the analogy, but the owner was spared the bother of having workmen around under foot until the end of time. I have been in churches that had been in use for forgotten centuries, and men who were baptized in them had been buried from them ages long ago, but scaffolding was around the towers, and hod carriers were toiling up ladders, and everybody thought this was the way to do it.

Great-grandfather, when he had his house ready to move into, still had one room to finish. But he just stopped work, and the room never was finished. That was the open chamber, so-called, and it was for the most part evidence that the old man got tired driving nails, and figured he had house enough without it. Unfinished as it was, if you could poll the folks who were born and brought up in the house, that room would come out ahead as the favorite room.

Its function has never been defined. It was the room in which the women sat or stood long, long hours and carded and spun greasy home-grown wool. It was the room to put things not needed right away but likely to be called for any minute. It was the room little boys went to on rainy afternoons and looked around to see what a little boy could do on a rainy afternoon. The cats always had kittens up there somewhere. It was a place to pile squashes, or hang seedcorn, or stretch curtains, or now and then to set up an extra bed and sleep the overflow visitor amongst the odds and ends.

There is one indelicate memory connected with the open chamber, and it has to do with the loose floor boards. The boards were never nailed down, and the temporary floor became immediately permanent. The ends of one turned up, another turned down. It was safe enough, but some people were skittish crossing as the squeaks and rattles sounded bad. Down below, in the kitchen, folks sitting at night would have their flesh creep when a rat ventured across the floor with a tomcat in his wake and made a noise like six horses racing on a wooden bridge.

Well, once in a while we boys were herded up there to sleep two or three on a cornhusk bed, while visitors usurped our places, and our equipment included a tin vessel known genially as a combinet. It was our practice, when using this device, to set it on a certain board with magnificent vibration qualities, and then stand up on the bed and see if anybody could recognize the tune. We boys, naturally, thought this was a more or less private entertainment, and supposed the orchestration was confined to the open chamber. But this was not the case, and as the amusement progressed everybody in the whole house became aware of it. It was not easy to figure out what caused it, unless in your time you had been a little boy sleeping in the open chamber, and if you had been asleep in the far corner of the house you would sit up as if a brass band had suddenly blared out *Hands Across The Sea* from under your bed. Speculation as to what caused this din would run through the family, and those who knew were too polite to say so, and those who didn't went uninformed. If anybody came up to look in the open chamber they found two or three boys sound asleep and utter quiet in evidence.

Another time, before my day, when the floor boards got a chance to show off, would be in spinning season. Grandmother and the older girls would go up there and get a couple of the old wheels going—the big wool wheels. One girl carding could turn out rolls to keep two spinners busy, and the two who spun walked miles upon countless miles back and forth on those rattly boards, with the vibration and hum of the wheels setting the whole house to throbbing. Grandmother was quickest at it. She would walk up to the wheel and put the wooden "finger" against a spoke and flip the thing hard enough so the momentum would carry the fliers while she backed off and fed the wool in. Pushing, pulling, feeling, smoothing—her nimble fingers would pass the carded wool in just fast and thick enough to make the twist, and she would walk up with the roving just in time to flip the wheel again and not lose the speed.

‡ 59 ‡

I have heard, and read, about such spinners in other homes in other places, and the story usually went that they had spinning songs they sang. This must have been pretty, and I am sorry our family didn't join in such a domestic vocalizing. I have never heard that anybody in our family knew any spinning songs, although they may have. The truth is that nobody with the true blood in his or her veins had voice enough to carry a tune, and our nursery songs were always sung in a doleful monosyllable that wasn't even a full note. For some strange reason none of us much has ever liked music, probably because in later years we didn't recognize the real thing when we heard it. Grandmother, who loved to sing and was always running through a hymn at her work, was notoriously single-noted, and even had difficulty in finding that one when she wanted to. This may have been the reason spinning songs were not employed in our open chamber, but I think the floor boards had more to do with it.

I don't think Billy Sunday's evangelical choir could have brightened that corner with song, because no matter what note you touched some board in the room was pitched the same, and it would jump up and shake itself with sympathy. The vibration of the two spinning wheels gave all sound the undertone of bagpipe drones, anyway, and it was folly to try the melody in that bedlam. What the women did, of course, was talk—in loud voices to counteract the surroundings, so by evening they had no voices at all and went around talking in whispers. The jabbering of the spinners also reverberated through the house, and people elsewhere couldn't make out any words, but heard them all. It is probably a good thing our women had no spinning songs, because the family probably wouldn't have liked them.

Once a cat had kittens in the open chamber, and one of them fell down between the studs and the chimney, and sat just behind the wall and the woodbox in the kitchen yowling as if it had something the matter with it. This presented a problem, as a defunct kitten abaft the woodbox wall is not likely to render a kitchen more and more enjoyable as time goes on. Kittens, around the house in those days, had slight value, if any, and disposing of a certain number every year was part of farm life. Mother cats are more energetic than necessary. Great-grandfather lay on his stomach up in the open chamber for several days, trying to catch the kitten in a noose of twine, with the mother cat roaming around over his head and shoulders trying to help. In the end he took down part of the kitchen wall and retrieved the kitten, after which he put back the wall, and the mother cat lugged the kitten back upstairs and it fell in the hole again. Great-grandfather retrieved it a second time, and not only plugged up the hole from above, but went around with great ambition and depleted the farm's supply of cats.

The open chamber could be reached from the front stairway, and it also had a back stairway which was always piled with things to be taken up into the open chamber. Insurance companies have appalling statistics on the injuries sustained because people step on something left on a stairway and come down on the back of their necks. Our stairs never injured anybody, in a permanent fashion, but hardly a day went by that somebody didn't go the length of them on one ear and bring up against the wall at the bottom with a noise like a drum. It wasn't customary for anybody to rush out into the back shed and see if injuries had been sustained—we simply opened the door and looked out to see who it was this time. I speak of this here in a general way—but relatives who read this will come around and show me scars on their heads, or speak of bumps more specifically. The day Grandfather came down the stairs with his arms full of preserving jars and met my father going up with the disassembled parts of his new bicycle, and they both stepped at the same time on a box of shoemaker's tools isn't likely to cause the insurance statisticians any merriment. Grandmother is supposed to have remarked that people should try to be more quiet while the baby slept.

The chamber itself was a sleep-destroyer in two distressing ways, if you were a little boy who didn't know too much about what went on outside your pile of blankets and covers. The chamber was very noisy on frosty winter nights when the cold pulled nails out of the walls. Some may not believe this. But it really happened. I suppose water would get inside the clapboards of the house, and would freeze so it tightened up the boards somehow. I do know that every little while, when the thermometer was down out of sight and the still cold night stretched from us to the stars, that there would come a report like a revolver shot, and I would lie shivering under my bedclothes with vague expectations of civil disturbance and blood flowing in the streets. The hollow old chamber would echo back and forth for a time, and then it would be still again.

The older folks explained that it was just the frost pulling out nails. When the pressure got strong enough, one of those old hand-fashioned nails that had been driven a century before, would let go with a blast and draw right out of the board. A half dozen such explosions and those who slept in the open chamber were in great trouble.

The other way the open chamber kept us awake was with the death-watch. This was some kind of a bug that got into the dusty old timbers and chewed with a great snapping of his insect jaws in a most methodical manner. It sounded not unlike a clock ticking just at the limit of hearing range, and in the still of the night it settled down most amazingly to the steady beating of a heart—your heart. No wonder the older folks sometimes attached dire significance to them, and connected them up somehow to the ebbing moments of time. Once in high school a boy recited *The Death of Benedict Arnold* in a prize declamation contest, and he stressed the refrain—" . . . and the death-watch ticked in the narrow walls . . ." Not all the children knew what a death-watch was, but I did. I'd heard them in the dead of a summer night, while I tried not to, ticking out the monotonous hours as they chewed through the great white pine timbers and presumably did nothing more significant than satisfy appetites. In the daytime I suppose they tick just the same, but you don't hear them so well. You don't pay any attention, anyway. But at night the small tick grows and grows until it gets to be a thunderous drumming, relentless and unceasing, mysterious accompanist, harbinger of nothing but a slow and lingering end. Years afterward I read about Browning's bishop who was dying slowly by degrees, and didn't know if he was alive or dead. I thought immediately of the death-watch in that old open chamber—that was the way little boys lay there with the pillows clamped around their ears, listening willy-nilly to that methodical tick —tick—tick—tick; the death-watch of Benedict Arnold: "Hours and long hours in the dead night, I ask 'Do I live, am I dead?' "

But it was a nice place, that old open chamber, and

everybody in the family will tell you it was pretty much their favorite room. I can tell you when it was best. It was in the early summer when the woodbine started again. Grandfather had a woodbine by the front door, and it climbed up to the eaves and thrust through the cracks of the boards into the open chamber. Then it crept along the timbers and festooned itself luxuriantly all over the room. Grandfather said it was nothing but a weed, and he wished somebody would find a way to get rid of woodbine, but I think we were glad he never discovered a method. He used to cut it back by spells, but it always seemed to grow better after that, and it continued to adorn the old open chamber and add greatly to the effect right up to the time of the fire.

ONE of our roosters used to get up and sit in a nest for hours at a time, so I am not alarmed at anything much, but I don't suppose a little boy around a farm needs to take his hat off to a rooster. An imagination is a great thing. While we were hauling out the logs for our new house, our lad took part with a pleasing mixture of fact and fancy which was at times confusing to everybody but him. One day I was down on my knees in the snow adjusting the draw-bar on the tractor, thinking to twitch some logs out, when a thunderous roar went by me in a thousand different directions.

It was just the lad making the most of a Saturday. He veered around the woodpile, gained on the dog, and came about under the cherry tree with a grinding of gears and all eight wheels locked hydraulically. He backed up with unbelievable power, the vibration of his machinery making my ears wiggle. "Br-r-r-r!" he said.

"What goes on?" I called to him; and then I added,

". . . Bill." Bill isn't his name. Bill is the name of the other fellow when you're engaged in juvenile engineering.

"Hauling out logs!" he said, and he shifted gears again. Then he added, ". . . Joe." Joe is always Bill's helper.

"Got a good day for it," I said.

"Yes sir," said Bill, and then so I wouldn't misunderstand he told me, "I got a high-speed motor here."

"Now that's something," I remember saying. "It saves on wear and tear. Look out you don't back into the corner of the barn!"

"Nope! Br-r-r-r-r!"

He pulled out with another load—a big load this time, so big he had to back and fill three times to get into the road. He hauled it around by the mail box and piled it up with a great deal of yelling back and forth among the two or three dozen Bills and Joes engaged in this mighty undertaking.

I'm thankful for my special six-way vision. It has allowed me to see things like the huge wheels, the heavy logging bunks, the red-painted cab, and the torrid exhaust that attests the great horsepower throbbing under the hood as activities like this take place on our usually moderate farm. Anyone else would see nothing but a little boy running back and forth with his tongue hanging out and a badly fagged dog stumbling gamely at his heels. And it isn't hard to see the enormous pile of logs —more than enough to build our house with, and all of it yarded and piled in minutes.

Some of the lad's pursuits call for extra sympathy. Lopping the limbs off the Balm of Gilead tree seemed to him the close equivalent of pruning a grapevine, and except for the discrepancy in variety he did a good job.

When he shoveled an acre of snow into the pigpen, it was easy to see he had successfully made a manure spreader from the toboggan and an old apple crate. And when he bored holes in the clothesline supports and stuck in clothespins, it was simply to find out if the sap were running yet. So it wasn't surprising that our winter's activities with logs and lumber in the far woodlot should prompt him to emulation and even superiority. So I worked on the tractor draw-bar, thinking it would be nice to harness this juvenile energy somehow. I could use a high-speed motor myself. I watched him go by again, every nut and bolt of his fine machinery urged to sustained efficiency. I figured it cost forty dollars just to blow the horn.

My own little 22 h.p. outfit isn't so much after all. It isn't even red. I started it up, all the same, set it to idling and got off to fetch the peavey and ax and chains. Then I got on again, threw it in gear, and waddled out across the field without throwing any snow around to speak of. I looked back and saw the high-speed motor, Bill, Joe, and all the logging outfit coming behind me as fast as his legs could make it. I idled the tractor again, and waited for him to climb up over the draw-bar linkage and get settled on the hydraulic arm.

"Okay, Bill," he yelled.

"Then here we go!"

"Joe," he said.

"Oh, yes—here we go, Joe."

We crawled up over the knoll, down into the woods. "I thought you were yarding logs," I said.

He said, "Aw, that was just play, I'd rather go with you."

So we went along, and we really yarded real logs, and every time I tried to reconcile a youngster's ideas of work and play I was interrupted. "Br-r-r-r-r!" he would say.

When I was in school a teacher we had showed us an interesting way to measure a flag pole without getting off the ground, and I made a note about it amongst my archives and thought it was a good thing to know. For thirty-eight years this teacher showed boys how to measure a flag pole without getting off the ground, and they all took the examinations and made out fine.

Then one day I had occasion to measure a flag pole and I dug out the old notebook and found the teacher had been wrong. She had been wrong four inches out of every foot, and nobody ever knew the difference. I made a note about that, too, so when an occasion arises to teach the lad something in the realm of geometry and physics I take a line that can hardly be termed paper-and-pencil. With several acres of our woodland being cut off for extremely practical purposes, I found plenty of occasions, and I made a practice of using that area as a classroom on every Saturday that offered the chance. On this particular Saturday our classroom had just been refurbished with a puffy snowstorm and it made a good time to consider leverage, and I suppose inertia and kinetics.

One thing I have found out about teaching, not as a profession but as a parent, is that the teacher has a boundless opportunity for self-improvement far in excess of that afforded the student. I think teachers sometimes miss that, because a lot of them seem to be going ahead without making the advances available. Somebody was talking on the radio a while ago, urging young folks to try out for the diplomatic service, and the kind of questions they are asked in examinations was gone into—presumably to show it wasn't too tough a grind. It seems candidates are asked questions as to whether or not the Tropic of Capricorn passes through New Zealand. This, it seems to me, is proof that certain educators are failing in their studies. I can think of a lot of things a member of the diplomatic corps ought to know, but the Tropic of Capricorn doesn't seem to me to be included. I do not know if New Zealand lies on that line, but if I wanted to know I should reach around and pick down the reference book I keep here for just such matters. As a teacher, entrusted with the task of choosing diplomats, I would know better than to put that question in an examination. I would rather include a question to find out if the aspirant knew how to look things up when it becomes necessary. I have long believed it is a waste of time to memorize any information that can be looked up, and have felt that teachers spend altogether too little time acquainting their students with reference works—a category that extends from the calendar to the entire contents of the Library of Congress and beyond. But if I did put a question about the Capricorn Tropic into an examination, I would hopefully look for a pupil bright enough to give me the same kind of an answer I gave when my English teacher asked which made the better heroine, Ophelia or Juliet?

Such questions do not belong in examinations, and have no more bearing on the subject than such doozies as which way is up, or how many mickles make a muckle. They do, indeed, indicate the wit of the teacher rather than sound the ability of the student. They indicate to me that the teacher has missed the point, and that the formula is sometimes less important than coming out at the end with the right length of rope to fly a flag. Perhaps I am wrong, but it doesn't seem to me a rule for measuring flag poles is much good unless it gives you the right length of the flag pole.

Anyway, the lad and I rolled a few logs in the exact center of a boundlessly beautiful world, and we studied inertia out where it lives. I showed him how a 16-foot spruce log, if still, likes to stay that way, but that once it starts to roll it takes a stout fellow to stop it. Stated academically by a teacher, in classroom surroundings, this might make an impression and probably has, but it seems to make a lot more impression when you have a peavey snaked out of your hands and sent swooshing into a snowbank. It is entirely possible to insert a small boy into a situation where this becomes noticeable, and a good teacher can fix it so he enjoys himself without being in danger.

It is only a step, then, to showing that a rolling log, when its momentum is properly combined with a pry and an inclined plane, can be made to do most of the work through a man's simple application of know-how. Is this a function of knowledge? Anyway, it amused both of us, and not only demonstrated a number of laboratory laws but also got the logs piled on the brow ready for a truck. We came back to the house in good appetite, and the lad explained to his somewhat bewildered mother the essential difference between a skid and a trig. Some day, in a classroom, he is likely to be memorizing the old rules, and will suddenly come to his senses and realize inertia is nothing but a spruce log rolling down a skid, or something you can overcome by light pressure on the other end of a pole. I think this will be good for him.

It is also good for me, because I find that instead of boosting and humping and tearing my heart out on these somewhat sturdy tasks, I study things out a little better, and convert everything to simplicity, and make an example where I used to make a job. The tricks of doing heavy work out on a farm are nothing new, and I picked them up back along from older folks who knew them too. I find that by making myself an instructor, I make things easier for myself. Most of all, I don't want the lad to wake up some day and find his teacher had a good formula, but the wrong answer.

Another thing, connected with having children around, is the problem of how to direct their energies into the right channels. Teachers who can't seem to get their children to do anything abound, and our town seems to be well supplied with a number of them who go around most of the time admitting it. This is quite a joke as far as I am concerned, and explains why I am not always sympathetic when organized education seeks me out for lamentations.

When we were getting ready to build the house we had to take down a birdhouse that sat on a pole, and it laid alongside the barn all winter. In the spring a bluebird came, and he was a liar. He sat on a wire and prophesied salubrious weather, and said we were going to have a balmy spring rich with blossoms and prevailing winds of a gentle and lovely nature, and I thought it was only fair to put up his house for him. The minute we got the house up it came off to snow, and he disappeared until sometime in June, and I haven't believed a bluebird since. But on that certain day it struck the lad we ought to put up the house.

So I dug a hole for the post, and then recalled I'd left a pail of water in the pen with the ram and it would be just like him to get his head caught under the bail and bunt the barn down. So I said, "Now get a big pile of little rocks to fit in around the pole so it won't blow

‡ 71 ‡

down," and then I went off to see about the ram.

I found him in good order, and then let the hens out for a romp, and filled the feed hopper, and looked to see if the rhubarb was up, and what with this and that it was a good half hour before I got back to the birdhouse, and there was a pile of rocks big enough to ballast an airplane beacon. The lad had cleaned up the whole hillside, and had rocks piled up that would take me a day to cart onto a wall. So I reflected, and found I had solved a distressing problem.

A few details remain to be worked out, but I think I have the answer in general. What I am after is a fool-proof method of harnessing juvenile enthusiasm and putting it to work in productive channels. I know it can be done at times, and I suspect it can be done always. If I can figure it out, we older folks can have our strikes, and take our vacations, and indulge our various whims and human enterprise will go on regardless. We won't have to turn a hand.

The whole trouble is that nobody has ever worked hard enough on the idea. The child-labor laws won't come into this, because my plan doesn't call for gainful employment or exploitation. It is merely to direct the energies being expended anyway. I have never set the lad at tasks beyond his years, but he staggers to bed every night exhausted, and every day he performs stupendous tasks that make me shudder at the thought.

I have seen three men with a team of horses and a stoneboat pick rocks all day and have less to show for it than the lad did when I came back. He didn't happen to be picking rocks, you see—he was fixing a birdhouse. If anybody, especially myself, had suggested picking rocks, there would not only have been a family towdy-row, but in an extreme case I might have been arrested

‡ 7 2 ‡

for cruelty to a child. I'm working on this detail of the problem, but I think it can be solved.

The same kind of thing happens all the time. One day he took down a pile of box-boards I had stacked carefully so I could make apple crates, and he moved the pile down behind the barn and changed it into a henhouse. He had the rooster in it to prove it was a henhouse. Strong men quail at my rooster, who has four-inch spurs like needles. It would take me a day to run him down. The lad ran him down and thought nothing of it.

One day he rode horsie-back all over the farm on the ram's back. My ram, except that he's wool-blind, has identically the same destructive power as the Pacific Fleet, and I do not ride on his back if I can help it.

One day, between school-out and supper, he took a monkey wrench and removed all the bolts from my three-row spring-tine cultivator. The dealer says it's a day's work for a mechanic to set one up, and although I'm therefore better than a mechanic, it wasn't easy. And it is commonly known that a youngster who can't keep his mother's woodbox filled is somehow able to move a whole woodpile out into the field and tier it up for a fort.

These things are everyday. All I need is some way to direct the foot-pounds into useful objectives and relate this energy to production. The day we moved the bluebird house was the first time these thoughts came to me, and it staggered me to think this sort of thing has been going on now for years and nobody but me ever saw the possibilities.

THE injection of a thing called a Quonset Hut into the nation's domestic scene is a result of world-scale planning of World War II, and it may or may not out-survive these winged words. It was, or is, built like a silo split up the middle and laid flat on the ground, with its rounded side forming the roof. Being of metal, it was considered airtight by those who went through the World War II period on a cultivator seat, and interesting if true. The Quonset Hut, after hostilities, became a surplus commodity, and numbers of them were conveniently arranged to accommodate unhoused persons just about the time we laid the keel on our new home.

It was our whim to avoid all appearance of modernity and to reproduce as nearly as possible the antique farm home of our ancestors. They, too, knew, we figured, and the amount of living in Great-grandfather's old house justified everything we could replace. A Quonset Hut, fine as it may or may not have been in the service of a world at war, was nothing we wanted. We wanted timbers and boards, and tight joints, and the things you can run your thumb along to see how the grain goes. So we felt sorry for the folks living in Quonset Huts, and wished in a distant sort of way that some of them, poor souls, might have had something better. Then came a disturbing piece of news. We read in a newspaper that some veterans of the war, needing housing, had been quartered in Quonset Huts down in some Massachusetts town, and were thus patronized by a righteously thoughtful community. This was all right until a no'theasterly blizzard swept our region, and snow blew into the Quonset Huts, whereupon the veterans started suit against the town for this uncomfortable deprivation of civil liberties. It seemed to us the question came on whether or not snow has any constitutional privileges under the law, and how much a person is supposed to take before he is considered damaged.

This, naturally, brought to mind the old house of ours, and how the snow used to blow into it. Our new home is insulated throughout and snow doesn't have a chance, but for some reason the old-timers never insulated, even though at least two good insulating materials were available here from the earliest times and were known to the hardy folks who first timbered houses in this vicinity.

The first homes here were log cabins, rolled up from the big pine logs, with dirt floors and a stone fireplace. Great-grandfather made one, and it was tight. After he laid up the logs he chinked the cracks with moss from the swamp, then fitted saplings against the moss, and plastered the whole gap with the sticky blue clay of our hillside. This made a wind-proof log cabin, and even today the same method is used now and then for lumber camps. Spending a winter in a moss-caulked log cabin is really an experience best left to woodsmen, as ventilation is not the best and wood is so plentiful nobody ever bothers to shut up a stove.

But the point is that Great-grandfather knew about insulation. When he came to build his house, from sawn boards and timbers, he forgot all he knew, and like all Maine farm houses of that period he built something which offered scarcely any resistance to the wind. In most of those old homes a good gale outside would let a farmer winnow beans right in his kitchen, and it was nothing to see a gust of wind come in at a keyhole and lift books off the table. Every clapboard had a crack, every board a slot and knotholes, and even the plaster was a special kind that accentuated the velocity and gave the wind extra incentive. The wind passed under doors, around windows, and even through the roof which would shed August showers. And in this fashion did our old home await the first blizzard of winter. When a real old he snowstorm swirled our way, the family saw something that must have been even better than life in a Quonset Hut.

Of course, some efforts were made to keep the snow out. They stuck wads of paper in the latch slots, and always pushed the nearest rug against the threshold of the door. One of our neighbors always used to nail blankets on the inside of his north windows, and said it helped. But snow came in all the same, and was an expectable part of life, and nobody around here ever thought to sue the community. A good wind would whip particles of snow against the sashes of the windows and hurl them between the glass and the putty somehow clear across the room and slam them against the baseboard. Some snow naturally blew right on outdoors again, but what remained could be shoveled up first and then swept.

I have gone to bed in the old house and slept snug and warm under my quilts and comfortables, and slept well in spite of knowing that by morning the foot of the bed would be piled with snow. So have a lot of people, and not because they forgot to shut a window, and some of them have reminisced in their ninety-fifth or ninety-sixth year and told me about it.

Uncle Timothy used to tell how he slept all one winter in the back bedroom with two hogs hanging from the beams, because that was the coldest place in the house. They'd slaughtered the hogs in early December, and they froze as soon as they were hung. The meat was still frozen the next April or May when they took it down to be cut up. Uncle saw no hardship connected with this company, but felt he was honored, as the hogs represented material wealth not every little boy could boast. He said on moonlight nights he could poke his eye out from under the covers and see the great glistening and ghostly carcasses hanging there with almost a phosphorescent gleam, and they would turn as the night progressed and even look a good deal bigger than was necessary. He said they swung on their cords because the earth was revolving all the time, and I remember he used to explain about gyroscopes, physical inertia, and several other natural oddities as a result of his observations during the winter with the two dead hogs. Uncle Timothy was given to that sort of self-instruction, and was so good at it I wonder how he never happened to think about suing the town.

One of the most amazing things in life is the amount of snow that can blow through a thin slit in a door. The pine in our front door had split, merely a weather-crack, and I suppose the thin blade of a knife would go through, but certainly not the big blade. After a storm we would find the whole front hall full of snow —not just a trace of snow across the carpet, but several bushels of snow blown away back against the stairs. And it would be packed down hard, so a shovel stuck under the middle of it would almost bring up the whole drift. Heat in a front hall would melt such snow, no doubt, but the only heat in our old front hall was what came in when we opened the door from outside, and Maine farm houses are notorious for leaving the front door strictly alone.

This made the back door doubly important, and all Maine back doors do, or should, open in. They should also open into a summer kitchen or a shed, so the winter outside will never come directly into the main kitchen when anybody goes or comes. After a snowstorm somebody had to open the back door, push the snow on the steps to one side, and then back up and shovel out the summer kitchen. The intensity of the storm was determined by the distance the snow had penetrated, and if the cream separator had snow up to the handle it was considered a normal precipitation.

Grandfather was strictly an indoors shoveler, and was never known to handle snow outside the house. He would tread it down on his way to the barn, and tread it again on his way back, and if the doors were plugged up he would swirl away enough with his foot to allow entrance. Nobody ever dared call Grandfather lazy, because his deeds were prodigious, so his disregard for snow was purely a philosophic approach. He felt nature had placed it where nature wanted it, and it was his duty to go about his business without interfering overmuch in the general plan. So after he had shoveled or swept out what blew into the house, he felt snow was no longer a domestic concern. Uncle Timothy was just the opposite. He made paths all around everywhere and had them neat and straight. The day I hooked up the new bulldozer blade on the tractor and began pushing snow around the door-yard was the day Uncle Timothy went out to the chopping block and cut up his old wooden snowshovel. He did it deliberately, and without a word and carried the pieces into the woodbox. He said if they'd had things like that before, even Grandfather would have made paths, and probably would have used it in the front hall.

I don't want to make this sound too Spartanish, because I don't think we people ever liked it any better than anyone else would. But it went with living in the old houses, and was one of the poorer features to balance off against all the good ones. Certainly we never tried to blame the snow on anything lesser than the divine scheme, and if our community really had any liability there-in, our forefathers certainly passed up a wonderful opportunity. If we'd only thought to sue, ours might be a rich and retired family, because I guess we've had as much snow blow in as anybody.

We've had to get along with the snow and cold weather that didn't blow in, too, and most of us have built up a rather strong feeling about winter. We don't mind winter half as much as we mind people who think it's a nice time, and if anybody wants to get me going, all he has to do is stand up and sing *Jingle Bells*. The song runs, "Oh, what fun it is to ride in a one-horse open sleigh." I object to that, because it is not fun to ride in a one-horse open sleigh at all, but it is a cruel, inhuman torture far more unpleasant than hiking the same distance through the snow barefooted. I would certainly rather sing about it than do it, but my experience in one-horse open sleighs makes it painful even to sing, and I have gone through life as a militant kill-joy who interrupts front-parlor harmonizing on frosty winter nights by stopping the music to relate what it is really like to dash through the snow behind a horse who is lean and lank, jingling as we go.

Radio singers, youthful vocalists who know nothing about the rigors of transportation in the sub-Arctic, foil me, for shutting off the radio can never instruct them adequately, and I suspect they are currently making too much money to take the time to retire into the country and have me expatiate on what I know about sleighing.

Possibly if I can communicate here some of the little-known pleasures of rural runners and those who ride, I may be doing a public service that will eliminate the singing of *Jingle Bells* by people who don't know a pung from a side of beef, although I imagine a good many old-timers will never forgive me the thoughtlessness of renewing an unpleasant memory.

Grandfather, with whom I did my sleighing, had a Morgan horse that he mated by times to whatever was handy, and the offspring were numerous and no two alike. Somewhere along the line he got a mare colt whose legs were like bean poles, and she could lope along our country roads with speed, abandon and delight. Her paternal influence equipped her every fall with a fur coat, so she looked in sleighing weather like a Shetland on stilts. She was supposed to be "broken," but Grandfather didn't always depend on dictionary definitions, and grooming her for a trip to town was a stable labor that Hercules was lucky to miss. Grandfather insisted on that much style when he went to town, although it would have been far easier to have brought out poor old moderate Tantrabogus, who was the off-horse of the team. He had no style, but he liked me.

Tantrabogus was too big for the sleigh, and Grand-father wouldn't go to town in the pung, so we groomed Colty while she beat her heels on the hickory planks behind her and whistled wildly through her dilated nostrils. Somehow the song omits to mention hitching up for the ride, which is part of the story, and I think it should be mentioned.

When we led Colty up to the wagon shed we always had to hitch her to the ring on the wall while we got out the sleigh. It was always frozen into the ground of the shed, and we had to chop and pry to get it out. It came loose with gravel stuck the length of the runners and would never slide worth a cent until we had gone half way to town. Colty had to hunch up in the fills and get it started with a bounding take-off. The way it scraped in this maneuver makes goose-pimples on my spine even now.

There was much formality in getting ready for this ride. It was three miles (and still is) to the stores, so Grandfather had to have a hot soapstone for his feet, bottles of hot water in his bear-coat pockets to warm his hands on, and a lighted lantern under the buffalo lap robe in an early attempt at centralized heating. Little boys who hid their frosted faces under the robe simply substituted suffocation for congealing.

Besides yelling at Colty, who didn't like to stand, getting ready included pointing her in the right direction. When we were tucked in, and our feet shared the soapstone, and the lantern was between us, and we had the molasses jug stuck to our boots, and the dog was appropriately stanced to bark us out of the driveway, Grandfather would slap the lines down on Colty's

‡81‡

drawn-up rump   we would get the most gosh-awful jerk this side of a Salem witch hanging. Colty's feet had been jammed into the dooryard snow, and when she let go she would slap us in the face with four of the hardest snowballs ever invented.

Thus stunned, with the wind out of us and the graveled runners making our hair stand up under our stocking caps, we would make the turn by the mail box into the highway with the dog yapping joyfully at Colty's heels and Grandfather executing a complicated strathspey designed to keep the lantern upright, the molasses jug intact, the soapstone in place, his pocket bottles safe, his robe aright, and Colty in some sort of general direction.

Naturally there were bells. One string on the breastband of the harness is now obsolete except on front doors in Connecticut. We also had a short string each side of the surcingle. Then each shaft had three bells ahead of the breeching strap hook, and Colty's special sleighing harness had a couple on the saddle, just below the check-rein hook. Then, and this was Grandfather's personal touch, he had two big team bells riveted into the whiffletree—a sopranner and an alto, each about half the size of the thing in the Congregational Church belfry. Colty's first jerk set these to going, and the only thing I've heard to match it is Quebec City on New Year's Eve when they hold the bellringers' picnic.

"Dashing through the snow" is a historical inaccuracy. Colty would dash about seventy-five yards, and then discover she had been inveigled into a trip to town. She would recall the warmth of the stable, and how she had neglected to clean up a wisp or two of hay, and how much fun it was to beat on the hickory planks. So she would stop abruptly and look back at us.

‡ 82 ‡

This came at the precise place where the pines along Small's pasture wall stopped, and before the hackmatacks began. It was an open place with a good sweep, and while Colty looked at us the frigid north wind, which had been coming for weeks with us in mind and had achieved its supreme nastiness, would play upon us with enthusiasm and effect. (The song neglects to speak of this moment, but I consider it part of the story.) So Colty would look at us while Grandfather slowly shifted the lines from his right to his left clumsy teamster's mitten, carefully arranged his bottles, lantern, jug and soapstone so he could lean, and reached for his whip. His intention was to touch Colty up and improve her ambition.

But Colty had been touched up before, and as soon as Grandfather was sufficiently off balance and had his jug in the most precarious position, Colty would lunge ahead again and run like a wounded deer as far as the schoolhouse. The schoolhouse was a point of indecision, because Colty was sometimes employed by one of our younger uncles to take the teacher home, and as far as Colty knew this might be courting day. Colty always looked back again at the schoolhouse, and when she saw Grandfather reaching for the whip again she would throw more snowballs, the jug would roll around, we'd grab for the lantern, and for a few hundred yards Grandfather would be yelling at Colty, trying to get an honest "holt" on the reins, and feeling optimistically for his soapstone.

We eventually got to Hinckley's Hill, jingle-happy, cold and joyless. Hinckley's Hill was a bad place and many a farmer had "spread" his horse by hastening down. Grandfather arranged for a decorous descent by gathering in the reins with stout arms and braced feet, so that Colty's mouth looked split clear back to her withers, and most of her fore parts were gathered back into her own lap.

She minced down the slope while we stiffened still more with the cold, and seemed much put out by this curtailment of her freedom. But when we had gone down the hill and were on the level, and the tight rein was relaxed, she always stopped. Grandfather never seemed to learn, but would reach for the whip, and then we'd have the sleigh seat jammed into our shoulders and go jingling on into the village.

But not laughing all the way, because by this time the soapstone was frozen stiff, the bottles no longer helped, the lantern had fouled the inner air and left it clammy and damp. If any part of us was not cold the rest of us was too numb to know it. But we jingled on, huddled under the robe, with Colty taking her own good time, people looking out at us from warm village front rooms, and hoping we'd make the hitching post at the Farmer's Union before our feet and noses dropped off.

Trading, with sleigh riders, was leisurely. Nobody could buy anything until he got thawed out. You couldn't even see until your eyeballs stopped squeaking. So Grandfather unwrapped his soapstone and put it on the ram-down stove, emptied his bottles in the sink, blew out his lantern, and backed up to the stove after the ancient and honorable custom of those who dash through the snow in a one-horse open sleigh.

Going home was easier, because Colty knew where her stall was. She'd unhinge her long legs and put them down with ground-gaining alacrity. Snowballs flew wide and high, the bells went crazy, and the wind blew

‡ 8 4 ‡

through us so the heat we'd absorbed in town didn't amount to Hannah Cook.

Soon we would come into the dooryard with our back-bones jingling, and would jump out gladly. Now comes one of the little-publicized sensations of sleighing —that unearthly illness that grips the pit of your stomach when you jump out of a sleigh with frozen feet onto the hard-packed dooryard.

Almost as bad is the sensation when warmth begins to come back into you, a soul-stinging sensation that makes quite an impression. You effect this wonder by sitting on the back of your neck on a kitchen chair, and injecting the rest of you into the oven of the range. That old kitchen wasn't always warm, and it did have a draft and snow did blow in, but coming in from sleighing made the comparative stifling heat a welcome sensation. The stove, to achieve peak efficiency, should be stoked with good upland hard cleft-wood, and should be jumping up and down at hot-biscuit pitch. No sleighing party is complete without a hot stove to bake in afterward for an hour or an evening. Grandfather always took a hot mustard bath as well, but like sleighing itself this cure has pretty much gone out with the ailment. It is, however, nice to know that our new kitchen would be able to take care of a sleigher on short notice if any of us ever got up courage enough to dash through the snow again.

A T the head of the back stairs, in the old house, was a little room under the eaves that I never liked. I had no reason for not liking it after I grew up, but as a child I didn't like it because of the numerous tales I'd been told about the tramps who had slept in it. It was the tramp room.

I never knew any of these wandering gentlemen personally, and it has been long-long since a tramp came by here. In those days the lumbering activities in the Maine woods brought many tramps into the state, it being a definition difference that a tramp will work for his living. Those old tramps were a clever lot, if you can believe the stories they told, and could turn their hands to anything they took a mind to. If they didn't take a mind to it, they just left and kept going until they found a task more suited to their desires.

Tramps used to come in winter just as much as they did in the summer. In those days the ice for New York City, and maybe other places, was cut over on the Kennebec River around Bowdoinham and Richmond, and tramps that came to help at this frequently came or returned by our road. Presumably they had the farm marked out, somehow, as a good place to stop, because most of them stopped one time or another. And while they were here they had this little room at the top of the stairs, which wasn't really a room at all, but just the loft over the summer kitchen and shed.

The first person I know about who had this room was the little Negro Grandfather brought home from the Civil War. Nobody now living knows much more about it than I do, as all we have was handed down from the folks who lived here at the time, but Grandfather did bring home a black lad that had followed him through the war as what we folks in Maine would call a chore-boy. He slept up in this tramp room for the short time he stayed at the farm, and years afterward somebody was poking behind a beam there and found a horse-card filled with the crinkly wool from the lad's head—he had brushed his hair with a stable card and kept his toilet article up over the beam.

Just where Grandfather picked the boy up we don't know, but it was fairly early in his campaigns. Grandfather's outfit was made up almost entirely of boys from around here, and most of them got wiped out. I think there were five from this neighborhood that finally came home after the war—which may be a historian's explanation of why New England and Maine declined in the late decades of the 19th century. This area has never got over the loss of its young men in that senseless conflict, and from things Grandfather told I don't think any of those who went away to shed their blood in southern grain fields had any acute sense of the fundamental economic causes of the strife. It was popular to go to the wars, and the boys flared up and marched away whole

companies at a time. Three, two, years later they strag-
gled back to the farm hillsides, and life looked different.
Too few of them came home as Grandfather did to pick
up where he left off, contented and industrious, to
round out full years of self-reliant success.

Grandfather used to tell his ornamented tale of his
homecoming, and however it may have been, we do
know this colored boy came home with him, trudging
along at his heels carrying an ax. The ax had been at
Gettysburg, all through the Wilderness campaign, several other noted battles, and everywhere that Grandfather went the little boy was at his heels carrying the ax.

There was a chummy, camping-out complex to
Grandfather's early days in the war, and he had several
home-town boys with him to enjoy things. Four of
them, Dan Small, Frank Farrar and one I don't remember, stuck together all along the way and shared their
experiences generously. Being farm boys, and therefore
ready-handed in any emergency, they took care of themselves when less resourceful mates fell into difficulties.
I have always thought there was something specially
Maine in the fact that Grandfather carried an ax with
him when he went to war. You take an ax out of a
Maine man's hands and he hasn't anything to do with
himself, but leave him axed and he is master in any
company. Maine people have done more with axes
than anybody else, and we still have thin-fingered folks
around here who can plane a board down smoother
with a hatchet than most people can do with sandpaper.

As the 16th Maine Regiment, Company I, moved
southerly, spreading destruction in its wake and accumu-
lating a wealth of stories for the coming posterity, this
boy attached himself to Grandfather. Grandfather had
won his sergeant's stripes by that time, mostly because

he knew how to write, and it was natural for the boy to pick out the boss. Also, the boss had a hatchet, and it gave the lad an excuse for being around. Caddying with the hatchet lasted until the war was over, and by that time nobody remembered where the boy came from. They figured he must be something like seven or eight years old, maybe nine and it didn't seem right just to pull up the tent stakes and come back to Maine and leave the little fellow to shift for himself in what wasn't any longer much of a countryside.

So the lad came right along with the troops, and eventually Grandfather got home here boy and ax and all. We still have the ax, a treasure properly esteemed. It chopped most of the wood used throughout the south by the bivouacking Company I, and was responsible for many a chicken stew or smothered beef, depending on what livestock the landscape had the most of. For years it was in the woodbox in the kitchen, just to chip off kindlings to start the morning fires. It happened to be outside when the house burned, and is still useful if anybody felt like using such an antique treasure for day labor.

For a time the black youngster was a curiosity, and even today this part of Maine is almost entirely without colored folks. Neighbors came and looked at him, and he served very well as an animated souvenir. But I gather the women in the family had their own ideas. It was one thing to send the young men off to free the slaves in distant states, but it was another to have the slaves brought back to live in the house and eat at the table. Perhaps we're too far from 1865 and '66 to judge the situation with candor—perhaps we're not. Anyway some of the women laid down the law, and Grandfather had to get rid of his mascot. In the meantime the little boy spent what must have been a frigid winter in the loft over the summer kitchen, and he must have had some good qualities to attempt even a hair-brushing in that refrigerated room. Knowing how our family traces things back, I imagine it was Aunt Aphi who hounded the poor kid to distraction with, "Did you wash and comb your hair?" every time he came to table. The one child ever to live in our house and own a fool-proof complexion to help him avoid cleanliness was probably washed twice over every time just to make sure. It must have been fierce for Aunt Aphi to have a boy around whose neck could be scanned and she still didn't know if he was clean. Probably poor, frustrated Aunt Aphi was the one who finally demanded the boy be taken away. I can hear her saying, "Give me a boy you can be sure about." So Grandfather took the lad to Lewiston and gave him to his captain—a Captain Garcelon, and what Captain Garcelon ever did with him we don't know. That was the family who gave us a governor afterward, and developed a tender regard for faultless pronunciation of the name, but to us he was always Cap'n Gassl'n, because that was the way Grandfather said it. I wish one of the Gassl'ns would tell me some time whatever became of the boy who combed his hair in our shed with horse cards. In exchange, I will tell them about the time their illustrious ancestor, a captain in the 16th Maine regiment, went swimming in a southern creek and had his uniform stolen by a Confederate lady who then sat on the edge of the creek and damned him until his ears were as red as a boiled Penobscot lobster.

The tramps who came and went and used this room didn't stay long enough to leave distinguishing stories, most of them, but a few did. The most notable of all of them was Dr. Thaddeus L. Coulongtin, who was undoubtedly blessed with some other spelling to his last name, but Grandfather was never very much on French and he repeated it always just the way he got it. He was sure of the Thaddeus L., but the last name was beyond him. Dr. Thaddeus was a quack of the first water, and came here with every policeman in Canada looking for him. He was one of the old school physicians who shook up some cinnamon and wintergreen in a bottle of swamp water and inquired what ailed you before he decided what it was good for. He showed up here one evening in apparent destitution and asked if he could have a place to sleep and some food for his demanding appetite in return for any small work that might be available. Grandmother fed well, and loved to put a tramp into an after-dinner slumber solely for the compliments she received from a new customer, but Grandfather was equally solicitous and saw that no tramp went too long without adequate exercise to settle his meal. Dr. Thaddeus stayed here a long time, sweating copiously and eating furiously. The man-hunt in Canada continued, but Dr. Thaddeus saw no reason to help the authorities by dropping hints. Grandfather came to know about it because months after he came Dr. Thaddeus was so well established here he told about it. He had conducted what amounted to a swindle, and was able to bury his profits somewhere in the Province of Quebec before anybody caught up with him. He had come down the old Arnold Trail on foot, mostly to satisfy a love of antiquity and to corroborate recorded history, and felt if he stayed here long enough and behaved himself he might some day feel safe in returning to Canada to retrieve his fortune.

It wasn't any tall story he told, for he had no point

in telling one. There was no need to impress the folks. He worked with Grandfather at whatever farm work came up, and took part in the family life with mutual satisfaction, and comported himself creditably in every particular. He didn't pass as a doctor in the community at large, and everybody called him Tad. He was good company, a good worker, and gave as much as he took. The folks were glad to have him around.

When he came he had a big suitcase, and long after he had become part of the family he took Grandfather up and showed him what he had in it. He had every kind of remedy for every kind of ailment mankind ever heard of, and probably some not yet discovered. He said none of them was worth a cent, and all of them were essentially the same ingredients, which was water and something to color it and something else to make it taste bad. He said anybody feeling mean didn't relish a dose of medicine unless it peeled the skin off his tongue and made him realize he'd taken something. Dr. Thaddeus was here for several years, altogether, and finally said his goodbyes and went away, and nobody here ever heard of him again. For years the family was hoping some news would come back as to how he made out when he went back to Canada and dug up his hidden treasure, but we never heard.

One thing he left was a case of dope for race horses, which was in a little pasteboard carton over a beam, and it stayed there for a long time. It had the directions on the back, and Grandfather said it took one bottle to a race, and you poured it down the horse's throat just before you started. It was 90% alcohol, and probably not much else, and the horse would run his legs off and win. Grandfather never showed it to anybody, particularly the women, because doping a horse is something far below our lowest standards around here. Grandfather said Dr. Thaddeus never told him about the horse dope, and his own notion was that for all his admitted crookedness, Dr. Thaddeus was too much of a gentleman for such knavery.

The horse dope, it turned out, was really powerful enough to win a horse race, and it was fifteen or so years after that when Grandfather found out. When Grandfather first found it, he pushed it back behind the boards so it would be out of sight, and then he forgot it. But years later a neighbor down in the next house but one, Nathan Spendlove, took to racing horses at the fairs, and did quite a good thing with it. He had two or three horses, and one of them wasn't so good, and he used to let one of Grandfather's tramps drive her. This tramp was the current occupant of the shed chamber, and after he had won two or three races, most amazingly, with this second-rate horse, Grandfather discovered the carton of horse-dope under the bed with several of the bottles gone.

Grandfather was between two minds—he was mad beyond description at the idea of anybody coming such a foul trick on a dumb beast, but he was also righteously curious as to how the stuff really worked. This called for cautious action—first, he must carefully ask the right questions, and again he must control himself until he found out. The tramp readily admitted using Dr. Thaddeus L. Coulongtin's amazing tonic, and said it was true —he'd found the stuff most fortuitously the night before his first race with Spendlove's horse, and he readily attested that the horse had won when everybody at the track had bet against her. Grandfather was furious. But the tramp explained somehow that he hadn't given the tonic to the horse—he had drunk it himself. Thus fortified, he drove a magnificent race, and he gladly endorsed the product. Grandfather sent the tramp away at once, and when he went he took the remaining bottles with him.

Another tramp who stayed for quite a time was a deaf-mute, and he had everybody crazy before they got rid of him. After supper he would sit around the kitchen for a few minutes, and then he would take a lamp and go up into his room. After he had been gone for a short time the family down in the kitchen would hear all sorts of voices up in the shed chamber—as if a dozen people were up there holding a discussion. The tramp had been around the place a month or so before this happened the first time, and it had the same effect as startling everybody. Grandfather went up right away, the first time, but when he got up there the tramp was sitting on the bed taking off his socks, and he looked surprised at seeing Grandfather. Grandfather came down to the kitchen again, and in a few minutes the voices were going again. There were all kinds of voices— women laughing, men talking loudly, and all mixed up. Sometimes you could hear more than one voice actually going at the same time. Nobody ever found out what it was, and when the tramp left they heard no more voices. Grandfather used to say the man was probably an actor gone crazy, and he was out tramping, and wasn't really a deaf-mute at all. But he stayed here more than a year, and never said a word to anybody, even when a horse stepped on him or Grandmother would hit him a clip with a platter just to see if he'd say ouch.

A good many of the tramps had mouth organs, and some had violins and different kinds of flutes and tin whistles. These made out better, because a tramp that could fiddle made an excuse for parties. It was wonderful to have somebody who could tune up now and then, and it was the only music our family ever had. Probably the tramps knew how to go about getting the most for their music, because it always happened the same way. One evening after a new tramp came there would be music from upstairs, usually with the tapping of a foot, and Grandmother would send Grandfather up to get the fellow to come down and play in the kitchen. From then out he was in.

But one tramp came and played a banjo and sang softly to himself up in the shed chamber, and when Grandfather came up he said he guessed he wouldn't come down. So he stayed up there and played all to himself, and he did it every night for an hour or so. Grandfather kept asking him to come down, but he wouldn't, and it went along like that for months. Grandmother finally insisted, so the tramp came down and played, but he wouldn't sing. His tunes were all rollicking good ones, the kind you can tap a foot to, and the kind you just naturally have to sing with right out loud. But he wouldn't sing, and Grandmother kept begging until one day he told Grandfather, down behind the barn, why he wouldn't sing the words. The words weren't decent. He had picked the songs up in places where they didn't sing nice songs, and he didn't know any songs fit to be heard by a family. Grandfather told Grandmother, and probably she wanted to hear them all the more, but she didn't ask again and finally that tramp packed up and went too.

It was, of course, about the time the automobile came in that tramps began to disappear from the scene. They stopped cutting ice for New York on the Kennebec, and times changed. In my day a tramp was not particularly to be trusted, and it seemed unlikely that a few years before that they were welcome visitors. But they were, and part of life in the old house called for a place to put up a tramp when one came around asking for a place to sleep and some work to do. In our new house we don't have any chamber at the top of the back stairs—not just the same. We have a finished room with a dormer window on it, and I suppose the nearest we can come to perpetuating the traditions is to open it up to a summer visitor now and then.

IF anything ever happens to the White Mountains, we'll find it a long time between drinks, but as long as New Hampshire is the next best thing to Maine, we'll have water. Our water comes from New Hampshire, and it must be said of the Granite State that they don't stint. Fortunately, we think, nobody over there has any chance to do much about it, and we doubt if the supply is ever rescinded.

This spring of ours isn't like all springs, but we do have a number like it in this part of Maine, one of them up in the neighboring town of Poland and quite well known. Our water tests up just as good as Poland Spring Water, although it has 142 per cent less advertising by volume and won't cost you quite so much to slake a thirst or two. The geological fact behind these b'iling springs of ours is interesting, but evident enough if you think about it, whether you went to school or not. Poland Spring is away up on a hill, and it stands to reason no nearby source is responsible for all that water. If it were, the spring would dry up in August droughts about every year, and George Lane would wish he never heard of Hiram Ricker. George runs the Poland Spring outfit now, and the Rickers were the ones that owned it and made it famous.

A lot of people probably expect me to run around and take credit for the success of Poland Spring, which is precisely what I am going to do. My own Grandmother, Rebecca, was a Foster from over toward Gray Corners, and when she was just out of high school she took a job teaching in the town of Poland. I suppose she was the first one in the family who ever finished high school, and from what I know of Poland a decided advantage in this position. In those days, which were back around the Civil War, teachers boarded around when they taught in a town, and each family with children in school had to put up with the schoolma'am for a portion of the term. Thus, in Grandmother's first year in Poland she came to live at the Ricker farm, and had all the little Rickers of that day in her school. It was Grandmother's whimsy never to speak ill of anybody, so we can't be sure, but she said many times in her life that the Ricker children were nice little things, and at times showed a tendency to be almost human. The Rickers as a whole, in those days, were reported to me as poorer than Job's turkey, and were simply a remote farm family trying to find out what God put in the hills of Poland that made them different from any other wilderness. They were nice to her beyond all the requirements of civil performance, and made her feel right to home. She taught in Poland several years, and always looked forward to returning to the humble abode of the Rickers up on the hill, an abode she re-visited a half century or more later and found the prevailing price up around twenty-five or thirty dollars a day.

‡98‡

Grandmother always took great pride in the thorough schooling she gave the Rickers, and felt her lowly efforts with the book and rod had indeed transformed the ordinary into the superlative. Long years afterward Hiram Ricker of the red whiskers sent his patent-leather coach and gray span down to Gray Corners to fetch his old school teacher up to the Mansion House for some creamed partridge and fourteen other courses, and he told her he was indebted to her exceedingly for her insistence that he memorize the alphabet. He said he knew of no single thing which had contributed so greatly to his general enjoyment of life, that it led to fame and riches, gave him poise among men, allowed him to correspond with his friends and cuss his enemies in a more learned manner, made him cognizant of current events as well as historical matters, and helped him beguile his leisure time. He seemed thoroughly satisfied, and after picking Grandmother a huge bouquet of sweet peas, delphinium, phlox and verbenna from the Poland Spring conservatory he sent her home in the coach and four with liveried men before and behind, and told her he would be most pleased if she would come again.

But it was not the alphabet that Grandmother taught the Rickers which did so much for them. It was how to be a water witch. She was the best hand with a green elm fork that Maine ever saw, and she could go out and find water when there wasn't any water at all. I would be tempted to believe the water witching business is completely hocus-pocus if it weren't for Grandmother, Poland Spring, and our own pure bubbling fount behind the barn. A water witch grasps the two forks of a crotch and parades around like a sybil in a trance, and looks like the biggest fool that ever lived. But all of a sudden they stop in their tracks, take on an agonized awe, as if in the divine presence itself only more so, and the end of the stick twists and turns and points downward. "Right there!" they always say, and if you dig you will find water.

Not always, because a lot of so-called water witches have sprung up now and then, and not all of them have the potent gift, and not all of them are always right. The maddest man in the world is the one who has engaged a water witch, dug in the right place, and has gone down close to a half a mile and come up with dry sand. It happens. I do not know what water witches say to that, but with Grandmother it never happened. If she said to dig, you would always find water, and if through lack of diligence you failed, she merely smiled patronizingly and pointed out you didn't dig far enough. With Grandmother it was not a profession, nor was it a gift to commercialize. She never volunteered to find water, it was only when folks had looked and looked and couldn't find any, and came to seek her help that she took over.

Some witches claim the kind of wood you use makes a difference. Grandmother hooted at that. The gift was in you, not in the stick. Anything that had bark on it served her purpose, and it was only a personal whim that preferred elm. Anyway, when she was a girl teaching school up at Poland, as I got the story, she sat in the kitchen one evening correcting papers, and overheard Farmer Ricker lament the dearth of water. He needed a little better supply than the one he had, now that the heifers were coming in, and he supposed he'd have to turn shortly and dig himself a new well. Grandmother didn't say anything that night, but as the discussion over a new well drew along for a month or more, she eventually told them that she had located several good wells in her time, and was of the opinion she had the gift of a water witch.

Thus the time came when she had all the Rickers out ranging the hills with forked sticks, and showing them how to hold the rod and how to respond when the "electricity" took a-hold. She showed them how it worked all right, and old Mr. Ricker got onto it in no time, and found he could pick a wet spot as well as anybody. Grandmother herself didn't do any searching beyond the dooryard, but there wasn't any water there, and after the term closed she up and left and never taught in Poland again. It wasn't for a long time that she heard about the Rickers' really finding water, but she was glad at the news and realized the family would never have to worry again on that score.

After Grandmother married and came down here to live she told Grandfather one day that the slope behind the barn was an ideal place to have a barnyard, rather than up above, because down there he would find a living vein of water and he'd never have to pump for the cattle again. Grandfather had boys growing up to do the pumping for him, so he didn't hurry about investigating, and it wasn't until he laid up the foundation for an addition on the end of the barn that he found out she was right.

He was hauling out big rocks, and yanking them around to make a wall, when a sudden stream, almost a jet, of water gushed up in his face. He was down about ten feet below the level of the ground, and was so struck with the outcome of the prophecy that he ran to the house and got Grandmother to show her. She wasn't at all surprised, and when he laid up the wall he fixed it so a pipe led the water off into a drinking tub, and our cattle have never had a drop pumped for them since. They lowered a big flat rock over the top of the spring, and as far as I know it wasn't taken off in about seventy-five years. We took it off when we built the new house, and dug a trench out to it, and laid in copper tubing. Our electric pump brings this water into our home, and while it tests up as I say the same as the more famous Poland Water, we wash dishes with it, and bathe in it, and wash the floor with it, and treat it just as if it were common stuff. Geologically the water appears to be brought to us in subterranean veins all the way from the eastern slopes of the White Mountains, a hundred miles and more away. Our spring never drops an inch in the driest summers, and no matter how much we use the level stays the same. When we were running the cement for the underpinning of the house, and had a concrete mixer going from seven in the morning until five at night, we hooked on the electric pump with a hose line, and the pump would run all day long without draining the spring a mite. It runs in even faster than we can pump it out, because when the pump is going the overflow pipe still runs into Grandfather's old tub just as it has for seventy-five years or more.

We still have the well in the cellar of the house, which was used in the old kitchen via a hand pump. We ran a copper tube into that, too, and have it connected up so we can draw from it by turning a knob. But that is just a well, although a good one, and in dry times it does go down so the old hand pump sucked wind. Anybody can have that kind of a well.

I claim I can see a difference in the two waters, but a lot of people say I'm crazy. Years ago Grandfather had a housekeeper who insisted on having water from the barnyard tub to drink, as it was a better water by far than the kind pumped in the sink. The children thought she was just making it up, to put them to extra work of lugging a pail of water up to her every day. One day they brought her two glasses of water and told her to taste them both and tell which was which. She tasted them both, and pointed to the one she decided came from the spring. "I can tell every time," she said. "The water from the well is flatter, don't have the life to it." But she was mad when the children told her both glasses of water came from the spring behind the barn, which they did. "Don't tell me," she said, "I can tell."

We think it was curious that Grandmother, in her lifetime, should have the honor of locating the two best springs in Maine, and we have never felt overshadowed by those who have the other one. For all the years we've had ours, everybody who ever developed a thirst out in the fields and quenched it at the barnyard tub has wished the spring behind the barn might be piped into the house. Away back they didn't have electricity and couldn't do it, and then they got the well in the cellar hooked up and didn't have to. When you're building a new house you might as well do everything right, so we went ahead and laid the pipe.

There is no chlorine in our water.

THE Saturday before we moved into the new house we had a terrible catastrophe. My wife was lifting the pot of beans from the oven, and the bottom dropped out of it. She held the handle with a holder, and the handle was still connected to the neck and shoulder, but the beans were on the floor. They were swimming in their own delectable juice and the shards were sticking up like landmarks in the breakers. The cat came running with investigative enthusiasm and was enveloped in a cloud of steam. She backed up ten feet and looked unhappy. My wife looked forlorn and helpless. She said, with extreme evenness and great fidelity, "The bottom dropped out of the bean pot."

We had bacon and eggs for supper, and it didn't seem like Saturday at all. I dished up the beans, scooped up the juice, wiped up the floor and took our Saturday supper down to the hens. When I came back the spider was hot, bacon was in the air, and she was cracking eggs. We looked at the pot, what was left of it, and we decided it had a fault in it, and as Saturday succeeded

Saturday the constant addition of patina, essence, sheen and glory got to be too much for it, and it popped a joint and the bottom dropped out.

Friday night she had picked over three cups of beans, just as somebody has every Friday night here since beans were discovered, and put them to soak. All day Saturday she tended them, keeping the stove humping and opening the pot every little while to add some water. At half-past three she took the cover off for a time, to brown the top with its crusted bonnet of salt pork, and by half-past five they were ready. She blew the horn as usual, and we came in from working in the new house to see what the Lord had provided. We customarily make guesses about what we'll have on Saturday nights. We guess roast beef, and pork pies, and lamb stews, and even milk-fed halves of roast spring duckling, and you can smell baked beans not only inside but outside for quite a distance. Finally we guess beans, and mean it.

So it wasn't specially funny when she stood there looking at the steaming mess on the floor, but the loss of the beans wasn't the catastrophe. That was just a disappointment, an unfortunate accident that necessitated a change in menu. The catastrophe involved the pot itself. You just don't bake beans in any old thing, and it takes years and years to work a new crockery bean pot up into something that will bake a decent bean. Anybody knows that.

Great-grandmother's old bean pot was lost in the fire, and might easily be the most valuable possession we lost that night. It was almost a home-made one, because it was made right up the road by Barker Brook, where once a potter had his kiln and made crockery from the bright blue clay. He was a whimsical cuss, they say, and advertised his business by firing a particularly decorative chamber mug with the householder's name on it. He would bring these around whenever a new family moved in, hoping this introductory gift would foster business. He made one of these thunder jugs for Great-grandfather once, a huge affair with shoulder straps so the old man could safely journey a-field during his frequent discomfitures. Great-grandfather remarked to the potter once about his trouble, complaining that he had to stay close-by a good part of the time, and the potter came down a few weeks later with his gift. It was supposed to be quite a joke. This potter also made Great-grandmother's bean pot—a great vessel that would easily bake three quarts of beans, and was originally tested out in the hot ashes of the hearth before anybody around here had a stove. As much as anything this method serves like an old beanhole—which doesn't necessarily impart any special goodness to beans.

A beanhole is just a hole in the ground, lined with rocks to hold the heat, and you get the rocks hot before you bury the bean pot amongst them. When you come back later your beans are done. The ashes of the hearth worked about the same for Great-grandmother, but she was glad when she finally got a stove. Between hearth and stove she also had a brick oven in the kitchen, and this was even more like a beanhole. She het up the oven, and put in the pot. My notion would be that a hearth is likely to prove better than either a dutch oven or a beanhole, because it seems to me like less work.

They tell me the Maine custom of beans every Saturday night comes from the awe the old folks held for the Sabbath. On Sunday you didn't cook anything, and a pot of beans left over from the night before fed the body without disturbing the soul. I do know that some

‡106‡

other parts of New England, such as Vermont, take their beans any old time, and like them just as well, but they are open-minded enough to have stewed chicken on Saturday night. Stewed chicken, around here, is now strictly Sunday dinner fare, and we have retained the Saturday night beans without keeping the good Christian principle involved. As to Boston, all I know is that every year we send baking beans down that way, and they send back the next year and want some more, and I figure they must like them. They say it's hard to find a decent bean today in Boston, but that isn't so, because we sell of lot of beans down there.

Anyway, Great-grandmother's bean pot never missed a Saturday that I know of, and it always got a boiling out afterward with baking soda and was carefully set away on its own special shelf under the cupboard. Then we suddenly had no bean pot, and an aunt came up bringing a new one just out of the store. She said, "By the time the lad gets big enough to eat beans, this one'll be fit to bake some in." She knew what she was talking about. She knew the pores of a beanpot take on a mellowing that comes from weekly bakings. It takes barrels of beans, gallons of molasses, whole saltings of pork, bushels of onions, and months of blue moons to fire the quintessence into a good bean pot. The hand of the potter, whimsical as he may be, can't work this miracle in his kiln. It takes the loving care of a mother to pick and choose only the right beans, and the right kinds of beans. None of your midget pea beans by a long shot. Nobody ever found out how to brown a pea bean, and nobody around here ever cared about trying. Our beans at their best are Jacob's Cattle beans, and it isn't everybody ever heard of them. Some old fellow who knew his Bible named them. Laban's cattle were different from Jacob's, maybe you remember—Jacob's Cattle were ring-straked and speckled and spotted. And so is a Jacob's Cattle bean. Some may hold out for cranberry beans and such, but I believe a Jacob's Cattle is the prettiest dry bean of all. It comes about the size of a good kidney bean, and some say it is a cousin. Kidneys are not regular fare around here, nobody seems to like them steadily. But everybody bakes kidneys now and then, and no home ought to be without them.

Right straight along, most people use either soldier beans, with the little picture of a soldier on them, or the old-fashioned yellow eye bean. There is an improved yellow eye, which never seemed to me to be any great improvement, and I don't recommend them if you still have some seeds of the old-fashioned. We like to stick with Jacob's Cattle, and don't feel we go far wrong in doing it.

But even the beans aren't all-important. It takes hot hardwood fires over a long period of time, and none but the old and established families really get the best baked beans. And it helps to have other things in the oven at the same time—potato-yeast bread, punkin pies, sheets of caraway cookies, Johnny-cake, and all such as that.

So the catastrophe struck, and Saturday night before we moved into our new home we were impoverished to the extent of one useful and fairly well broken in bean pot. We started life anew, sort of, and brought into the new kitchen a brand, spanking new bean pot from the store, which was shiny and untarnished, and wasn't worth a cent. We began even, and I suppose succeeding generations can tell how old their house is by how good their beans are.

When we went to buy a bean pot, we found the

‡108‡

latest thing out was a steel one, highly polished and looking like something fine. We didn't buy one, although the man said we wouldn't be able to tell the difference. That's all the man knew. And it isn't wholly because principle is involved. One day a man down at the village asked his wife why she couldn't bake beans as good as my wife's. She was sore about it, but every Saturday he would complain that his beans weren't as good as the ones he had up at our house. His wife finally asked my wife, and mine said, "It's the fire. You can't bake beans in an electric oven."

They find their sparkling electric range has a number of advantages our wood range can't boast, but it seems to us a fine stove in the kitchen is a poor substitute for good beans in the dining room.

So I'm not so sure we couldn't tell the difference between a crockery pot and a steel one. We didn't want to take a chance. If a steel bean pot bakes better beans than a stone one, all I can say is I don't want any better beans than come out of our traditional vessels.

Uncle Timothy used to despise the annual job of threshing beans. He did thresh them, but it was under protest. He called the flail a "poverty stick" on the grounds that nothing was worse than being so poor you had to thresh your own beans. We still thresh our beans by hand, although flailing, like scything, is somewhat a chore that dates you. The flail is two sticks joined with a swivel, and you swing one in an arc so the other comes down with a bang on the pile of bean vines on the floor. After you have hit the vines enough times, you have knocked the dry beans out of the pods, and you can pitch the vines away and leave the beans in a heap on the floor. They still have dust and chaff and a good share of dirt amongst them, but the wind blows around here often enough so we can winnow beans in time for any Saturday.

It is considerable fun to watch a novice swing a flail. He grasps the handle with malice aforethought, brings it back up, and over and down with strength and abandon. The idea is to lay the thumper out at full length on the floor. What he really does is fetch himself a smart wallop behind the left ear and set the shingles on the roof to yapping and jingling in a manner most amazing to hear. Those present, not being tuned to the symphony, carry him out in the open air, loosen his shirt, and wait to hear his first remarks. When mastered the flail is a useful instrument, and it doesn't take long to pound out the year's crop of beans. It makes a good job for rainy days, and if we had a power threshing machine we'd finish up the beans in no time and then have nothing to do in bad weather. But when the flail is in the hands of anyone but an expert it becomes a menace. Since threshing beans is best done with company, it is customary for two men to work at it, standing opposite each other in such a way that one man's flail comes down within inches of the other's nose. A miscue makes for uncomplimentary remarks, and a certain amount of noise which disturbs folks in the house. They tell me it sounds like a dull and heavy thud, but it seemed to me more like being inside a galvanized bucket someone has hit with a rock.

Anyway, really enjoyable beans are not a simple thing to prepare. They start in the spring with the planting, and follow along through the months. And the cooking itself is nothing you do quickly, at the last minute before eating time. Great-grandmother's recipe, which was hand-written in the old book that got burned, paid full tribute to the time required, for her recipe began, "Friday night pick over two cups beans . . ." It was never Tuesday, or Thursday—and it was always Friday. She regulated each Friday night by the number expected for Saturday night, so sometimes she used three cups, sometimes she filled the pot clear to the brim. The beans were put on the back of the stove to soak, and before bedtime the kitchen was rich with that beany smell so promisory and hopeful.

The recipe then skipped to Saturday morning about ten o'clock, and said, "Put a good-sized onion on bottom of pot. Put in beans. Add ½ cup molasses, tblsp. mustard, 2 tsp. salt, piece lean pork, cover with boiling water." Then Great-grandmother stoked the fire all day, kept water over the beans until the middle of the afternoon. In the middle of the afternoon she would let them boil a little dry, which browned them up good. After she thought they were dry enough, she would pour water on again, and the pot would sizzle, a cloud of steam would pour out in the room, and each and every bean would assume its rightful share of essence and power. It was, indeed, a pot of beans—but baking them is predicated on the individual bean. One hard bean can spoil a whole supper. The whole is no greater than any of its parts.

Perhaps you wonder how we happen to remember Great-grandmother's recipe when the book was burned. Great-grandmother wrote that when she was fourteen years old, and she probably never looked at it again. Our women bake beans, not from recipes, not from memory—but from instinct. Give them a box of wood, a bag of beans, a shelf of ingredients, and a pot worth using, and they'll wind up the week with a steaming bowl of baked beans well worth all the nice things I've said about them.

THE old folks must have felt good when their first winter shut down around them, and they knew they were the only family in miles and miles with sawn boards between them and the weather. The conveniences thus afforded were numerous, and they also found the first house in an area has obligations toward more rudimentary neighbors.

There weren't many neighbors then. A trapper who had moved in six miles away lost his wife and left, a bitter piece of news for Great-grandmother. It was nice to have another woman handy, and she would be missed. After that a few settlers came in down around the falls of the river, and some of them stuck it out. The grist and saw mill was heralded as useful, and Great-grandfather had logs on the brow before they got the shafting trued up. Probably the little lady was twitting him about keeping house in a cabin, and the truth was that Great-grandmother herself was no slouch with an ax, but could keep going all day with her husband.

Sometimes I mention this to my wife, but she feels it is not a topic of mutual interest.

Anyway, there did come, the summer of the building of the old house, a new neighbor who was privileged to stay and become an ancestor, town father and legend. He was Amos Dearing, another man grown in his 'teens, and his wife was much older than he, a widow with two children who could give Amos as fine a tongue-lashing as anybody around here ever got and lived. The story is that she made his life miserable, and the few folks who were around here to know about it felt sorry for him. Amos larrupped around that summer and laid up a log cabin and went through the terrific work necessary to being ready for winter. From dawn to dusk he didn't sit down except to his meals, and while everybody noticed he did first rate, his wife lectured to him constantly about how his indifference to accomplishment was depriving her of comfort and convenience. Her efforts rewarded her, because they said by cold weather she had the best set-up any of the pioneers had enjoyed, and Amos had done twice the work for her that any normal husband would have done.

So that particular winter shut down on both the big frame house up here on the hill and the snug cabin down toward the stream, and the winds came and the snow blew and Great-grandfather commented on how mild it was when the temperature got up around thirty below, and Great-grandmother stoked her big brick fireplace and gave thanks for the comforts of modern times.

Amos and his wife stoked their fireplace too, a great square arch made with stones from the brook and plastered together with blue clay. They planned on building a nice new home some day to help while away the time—and as a matter of fact they did build a huge brick home. It burned long ago and has been demolished. Nobody ever tried to build it again. And one morning when the wind hugged east so it would sharpen a scythe and the sky was ashes and lead, Amos and his wife arose from their comfortables to find the hearth cold. Their fire had gone out during the night.

Some of this was hard luck, some of it may have been inexperience. Great-grandmother claimed she never lost a fire in her life, and never had one she didn't want. Banking up at night was a solemn ritual and much less work than kindling a new fire in the morning. The woodcraft manuals describe how simple it is to make fire without matches, but the old folks were glad when they could get a card of Portland matches now and then to save wear and tear on their flint and steel. When as a last resort they had to get down on their knees and spark some tinder into flame, they did it without any self-praise for their skill.

The trick to keeping a fireplace alive was in the backlog—a word that has come over into our speech without everybody's knowing just what it means. The backlog was green wood and it was not supposed to burn right away. It was rolled in back on the dogs, and you kindled the cooking fire ahead of it. You added dry wood to the fire when it was needed, and after a time the green backlog would dry out and begin to burn with a flame. While it only smouldered it gave a bounce to the heat, but once it began to burn you had to roll it ahead into the fire and put in a new backlog. Soon the old one would be consumed and forgotten, and housework went ahead.

At night the coals of the day's fire were pushed into a pile against the backlog and ashes were heaped around them. If the tiny vent at the top was neither too large nor too small, the coals stayed alive all night and it took only a moment to blow them up in the morning and have breakfast coming. We've heard a great many times how carefully Great-grandmother did this, not kneeling as a man would, but bending over from the hips like a woman so her head was in the ashes and smoke.

So Amos and his wife failed somehow to keep their fire going, and their cabin was coolish. His wife spoke about this condition, implying it was not the kind of good-morning coziness she was accustomed to, and she chided Amos for his disrespect of her welfare. She suggested he get busy and start up a small glow, something that would bring the temperature up to the minimum required by all well-bred pioneers.

Amos attempted so to do, and struck his flint on his steel until his ears rang like sleighbells, after which he struck the steel on his flint until they rang again, after which his wife assisted by telling him what she thought of the matter and then berated him because he stopped to listen. The morning sky, the kind succeeding generations have come to associate with impending howlers and drifts over the elms, now shut down into a ripper. I can not speak too highly of one of these disturbances. It not only was worse than anything we have nowadays, it was worse even than that, and I know because the old timers have told me so.

In those days the winters were rugged, and Great-grandmother said the worst storm she saw in her eighty-eight years was the one that week when Amos lost his fire. Poor Amos was able to work up a sweat by dint of exercising his flint and steel, but he wasn't able to communicate any of this to his wife, whereupon she stated that if he thought he was going to warm up the cabin by slatting his hands around he had another think coming. The day, we may assume, was not a cordial one in the Dearing family.

But the day passed. Mountains of snow piled up in the little clearing, and a bitter wind sifted it until you couldn't tell one flake from another. Mrs. Dearing took herself back to bed at intervals, where she had made the children stay, but occasionally she would arise to view the unkindled hearth and point out to Amos that although he might have contrary notions of his own, the truth was that so far he hadn't done much.

Now would have been the time for a boys' camp counsellor to step up and demonstrate the ease with which bewildered woodsmen touch off a cheery blaze. Now might a match have come in handy. But when the dying winter day wrapped its draperies about it and hauled in its head, Amos was still trying to draw fire from his tinder, and he had blown enough to sail a fleet around the Horn. At this point he decided neighbors must be for something, so he set out for our place to see what we could do for him.

Great-grandfather and Great-grandmother had long since banked the embers on the kitchen hearth, and taking off their mittens had gone to bed remarking proudly that this was some different from the old days in the cabin. The wind swirled cutting snow against the panes of their bedroom, but they lay snug, and all the perverse world was held at bay outside their newly fitted pine and spruce. Then the dog roused up from his bed in the snowbank outside and barked himself inside out, and they wondered what might be prompting this to-do. Then somebody kicked the dog so he ran yipe-yiping off into the woods, and there came a thumping at the back door.

‡116‡

Before Great-grandfather got down into the summer kitchen Amos had pushed open the door and come in, snowshoes and all. He stomped his feet before he took off his snowshoes, to get the snow off them, and he stomped them again after he took them off, to restore circulation. His fur cap was a peaked drift of snow, and his whispers hung with hoarfrost and rime. Great-grandmother had come down to see and now she poked up the embers and blew a fire while Great-grandfather was thawing out Amos and trying to find out what calamity had brought him thither.

Amos simply wanted some fire. He told what a wretched day he had spent, saying that he thought his wife hadn't added much to it. He didn't seem to be in too great a hurry to get started back, but backed up to the fire and absorbed all he could of it. They discussed fire-making and keeping, and Amos got a few pointers and tricks. At length he got back into his heavy clothes, pulled on his leather mittens, and was ready to go. Great-grandfather laid some cold ashes in the palm of Amos' right mitten, and then tonged a fairish-sized glowing coal in the ashes. He poured more cold ashes over the coal, and then Amos clapped his left mitten on over the top. They tied on his snowshoes, held the door open, and Amos clambered up and out for his trip home. It was down-hill against the wind and through dense old-growth forests, in a night made black by the driving white. Great-grandfather and Great-grandmother put their fire under ashes and got to bed again, and then lay listening to the storm and wondering how Amos made out.

But the story ended there—Amos got home, bringing fire off the hill like Prometheus himself. He stumbled a good many times, but he held his hands cupped before him until his shoulders throbbed down to his kneecaps. At home, he blew up his coal and started his kindlings and piled great logs on until his wife got up and told him he was wasting wood. After that, he always kept a fire alive, and when he was an old man he used to bet the young fellows they couldn't walk two miles on snowshoes with their hands cupped before them. They said he never had to pay off.

But Great-grandmother laid the story by as an example. After Amos got his big brick house built, a bigger one than ours and much more elaborate, Great-grandmother used to remind him that he owed it all to her. It was her coal that kept him from freezing to death, she said, and it probably was.

GRANDFATHER used to laugh about a woman down the road who had a patent method for keeping her cooking from getting eaten up. She would serve a skimpy little bit of pie, and when those present had politely broken it into two or three pieces and consumed it, she would enthusiastically offer, "Now if anybody wants more pie, I got plenty more right at the foot of the cellar stairs." Nobody had the nerve to make the poor creature go away down cellar to bring up more pie, and so this woman was able to go for days and days without making a new one.

It was equally true that her family went days and days without eating a new one, and we folks around the old farmhouse always felt sorry for them. Because pies were a regular part of our life and we had all kinds at all meals in any quantity the women felt good for us. Mince pie was supposed to sit heavier on our stomachs than apple or berry pies, but custard pie was something we were allowed to eat until Grandfather could look over and see it running out of our ears. He would point this out gravely and up to a certain age we youngsters really thought it could happen.

I'd like to know how many million pies were baked in the kitchen of the old house. I'd like to know how many million *custard* pies were baked—how many eggs it took to make them, the cords of wood the old stove burned to brown the tops, and the manifold happy expressions that sat around the pine table. These expressions were on faces that got smeared from ear to ear and around back of the neck so mothers had to wash them, and they were on patriarchs who got up and washed their whiskers at the sink afterward and went to their post-prandial naps with the resigned air of angels in the shadow of the throne. Custard has always been the favorite, but nobody in our family has ever scorned a likely-looking pie until it has been eaten, no matter what fruit or mixture held the crusts apart.

I think myself the punkin pies Grandmother made deserved more eulogies than we have given them, but the truth is we took them so much for granted nobody ever thought of getting up to make a speech about them. The punkin pies were also something we had pretty much to ourselves, although now and then I run into somebody who had a Grandmother as smart as mine. Most people who didn't have a smart one are going through life thinking punkin pies are round, and you can actually buy canned squash in the stores with a printed label that gives the recipe for pumpkin pies. You may be able to make a pumpkin pie from squash, but you certainly can't make a punkin pie from anything but a punkin, and I hope the proofreaders are on my side. Most important of all, though, you can't make a punkin pie unless you have a bakersheet.

Grandmother's bakersheets were eighteen by twenty-four inches, which is a sizable pie when you get situated so you can see across it the long way. They had sides on them a full three inches. The oven in the old stove, naturally, would take such a pie plate, and a bright sun set on American edibles when they stopped making stoves that would take two bakersheets, a pot of beans, four loaves of bread, and whatever cakes and cookies and Johnny-cake a woman happened to be running through on a Saturday morning. Modern women who have to have a small bean pot to fit the oven would have marveled at Grandmother's taking out the bread, cakes, cookies, punkin pie and assorted other items so she could reach in back and baste the turkey.

I suppose a bakersheet isn't all-important, and that some women might make a fair pie in another shape, but we grew up with square ones, and my contention is that they taste better that way. But one thing absolutely essential to a decent punkin pie is a punkin. Those big yaller kinds they have southerly with a flannel lining don't have the right pertness, and the little sugar pumpkins they advertise so highly in the seed catalogs aren't much better. It takes too many to a pie. What we had were the old-time cow punkins. These real punkins still flourish around here, and a man who has raised a quantity of them feels he has done something to improve the moral outlook of his family. They go up to seventy or eighty pounds, and I can prove it, and when a man gets one over a hundredweight he gets hopeful of a blue ribbon and takes it to Topsham Fair. These punkins have over a bucket of seeds in them, great big seeds you can step a mast on and make a toy boat, and I've done it. Grandfather always kept his biggest one for seeds, and dried them on a copy of the National Tribune up on the top shelf of the stove and hung them in a little cloth bag from a beam in the open chamber so mice couldn't steal them. Every two or three days during the winter Grandmother would call for a punkin, and chop it up with her kitchen hatchet and set some of the children to peeling it, saving the seeds for Grandfather and the skins for the pigs. Then she'd put the chunks (which she called *junks*) into her thirty-quart kittle and boil them.

Her secret was to boil it dry. She'd put only enough water in to keep the punkin from catching on, and she'd boil it until it was tender and all the juice had come out of it. It was done when it began to catch on some, and then she'd strain the pieces through a sieve. I've seen women try to make a punkin pie with a runny mess of punkin that went through the sieve on its own hook, but Grandmother always had to force hers through, it was that dry. She used to make her small pie with eight cups of punkin.

Next she took eight eggs and beat them until they'd yell uncle. Some people say you have to boil the milk, but you don't. You want eight cups of milk. That's two quarts, and nobody cares whether its homogenized or not. To hear some people talk you'd think milk isn't any good until it gets educated. Then you want two cups of molasses. That's a big problem in these days, because nobody seems to sell real molasses any more, and people wouldn't know it if they saw some. The old molasses came in a barrel and was a blood relative of cane sugar. You took a jug with a string looped through the handle and went to the store with it. Canned and bottled molasses was yet to be thought up, probably pending the discovery of the ingredients and the process for making it. Grandmother measured the molasses in her tin cup, and wiped the cup out most unhygienically with her index finger. This was quite a thing to watch. She would then wipe her index finger with her other index finger, gradually working the heavy, sticky, brown syrup off over the end of one or the other, and then paring the tip clean with a stroke of a kitchen knife. My own idea is that something in Grandmother's fingers went into the pie with the molasses that way, but others tell me it was just the molasses they had in those days, and even Grandmother couldn't do her old-fashioned job with present-day impostors.

Anyway, you add four teaspoons of cinnamon, four teaspoons ginger, and two teaspoons of salt. I say two teaspoons, because that's somewhere near it, but Grandmother actually added the salt by reaching into a crock and taking out in her hand what she thought was the proper amount. I imagine that in fifty years she didn't vary the amount by a grain one way or the other. When she got all this in the bowl she would mix it and mix it until one arm was ready to drop off, and then she would mix with the other arm.

The shelf in the old kitchen, where this work went on, was too high for us children to look to from the floor, and standing on chairs was not considered too safe. We could sit on the shelf and watch if we kept our feet down. Grandmother was resourceful in this, and had long ago found out how to keep children from resting their shoes on the edge of the shelf, looping their hands around their knees and taking life easy. "Feet down," she had said several times over once long ago, and then she had thought of a cure. She got an alder switch, and kept it beside the flour barrel. We children were supposed to hold the switch, and whip our dirty, nasty old feet if they so much as dared come up onto the bench. I can remember cutting my legs almost off at the knees, and remember how Grandmother would smile at me as if I were mastering a most distressing problem.

While I was mastering it, Grandmother would roll out the dough for the pie. She would roll and roll, and then would back up over the sheet of dough and wind it around the rolling pin. Then she brought up the eighteen by twenty-four bakersheet and deftly unwound the dough over it so it fell neatly into place. A couple of pats at each corner, and then she'd run the rolling pin along the top so the pressure would cut the dough off flush. Sometimes she would crimp the edges, but that was unnecessary as far as eating the pie went, and she knew it.

Next the mixture was poured into the crust, and the whole thing maneuvered into the oven. Grandmothers used to tell if the oven was right by the color of the flue, or if things on the back cover scorched, but nowadays they have thermometers and I think 375° might be about right. After she got the pie in the oven, Grandmother would usually pour a little more mixture in, to bring the tide in full like Fundy in spring flow. If the oven is het right you can allow pretty near an hour for best results—you go by the color and the smell, and I don't think a really good pie can be made without a dozen or so children peeking over your shoulder as you stoop to look in at it every little while.

A pie of this area has to be sot to one side to cool a spell, but it isn't long before some child has teased you into cutting out a corner. The corner piece has crust on two sides and is a wonderful thing for grandchildren, but it is well to remember a bakersheet has only four corners, and this limitation might cause trouble in large families. We had to take turns.

Once in a while I run into people who say they

would just as soon have another kind of pie, and when there is punkin pie on the table, I'd just as soon they would, too.

I don't want to convey that punkin pie is my only love. There isn't a pie filling we haven't had hot out of the oven, or a day old. They seldom lasted beyond the one day, and in our old kitchen no woman ever spoke of baking "a pie." They baked pies. The baking of mince pies was the most prolific baking, because sometimes they would bake a whole winter's supply. Not always, but every little while the right accumulation of aunts and sisters would be around the place, and somebody would suggest baking some mince pies, and they would turn out dozens upon dozens of mince pies. All they lacked was the endless belt of the modern baking factory. One woman mixed dough, another rolled it, and so on. Then they would put all the pies in the little screened cupboard in the cold summer kitchen, and they would freeze up as solid as the stove covers. Women with freezer lockers might like to know frozen foods were common in Grandmother's day, when the stiff Arctic winds brought the temperatures now provided by power lines. Weeks or months later a frozen mince pie could be warmed in an oven, and it came to table as fresh as the day it was baked.

The apple pies in my life have been too numerous to recount with individual attention. Yet each received that attention at the time, and I don't remember that I was too fussy what kind of apple they used as long as they put in enough. The apple pie season used to be perpetual, but by the time I came along so many other fruits were in the market the year 'round that the women had given up dried apples, which left an apple hiatus from approximately June to August. I have had dried apple pies, and thought they were wonderful. Home economics experts on the radio today make sarcastic remarks about dust and flies, and indicate dried apples of a century ago were vastly inferior to dehydrated apples of the present. I think they are wrong, and mostly because apples long ago had identity, while apples today break down into two major classes which include McIntosh Reds on one hand, and everything else on the other. I don't know what kind they dried, but I'm sure Grandmother knew and could expatiate knowingly on which kind dried the best.

The apple pie season began propitiously on the first day of August. Not the second, nor the thirty-first of July. On the first day of August somebody would bring up a hatful of Yellow Transparents which hadn't quite reached the point of having brown seeds. Brown seeds mean the apple is ripe—so our First of August pie was always a green apple pie. It was, rather, a greenapplepie, one word indivisible. I have no doubt that God prefers greenapplepie to any other tidbit, because nobody with His discernment would miss a chance. I think Heaven's biggest day is the first of August. But greenapplepie is not strictly an apple pie, and a little later in the month we got yellow transparent pies that came from brown-seed apples, and the apple pie season was definitely on. The yellow transparent is just an opener, however, because almost anything except a Ben Davis is better. Nothing is worse than a Ben Davis except a Sahara sandstorm. The nursery catalogs have wonderful things to say about all the other apples, but all they can say for a Ben Davis is, "The best keeper known." A Ben Davis not only keeps through its lack of enzymes, but because nobody in his right mind would eat one when anything else is available. Anyway, the

Red Astrachans came next. These tart, acid summer apples were as abundant as manna in the wilderness, and no country boy went anywhere without pockets of them to stay him until his business brought him under the tree again. Only one thing is better than Red Astrachan apple pie. That is Red Astrachan apple pie with just a dash of rich, ripe late-August blackberries worked in. No able-minded human will disagree with me on that. We used to eat one for dinner, hot from the oven, and then watch the older folks go to the sink and wash blackberry seeds out of their false teeth, pumping with one hand, it being well known that Hell hath not torment like a blackberry seed under an upper plate.

Grandmother, and all the other women we've had around here, knew which tree to go to next after the apples from the last one were gone by. The fall was a glorious succession of Dutchess, Wealthy, Twenty Ounce, and all the others, and around the table we sat with satisfied stomachs and questioned if Dutchess made so nice a pie as Wealthies, or either so nice as Twenty Ounce. Then we had pies made with Snow Apples. This country is full of people who were little boys and girls out in the country, and every fall at about Topsham Fair time they get hungry for something and don't know what ails them. A certain number of them happen to be around here each year at the right time, and we help pay the taxes by selling them Snow Apples. People like that generally suppose that all the old-fashioned kinds of apples passed out of existence when the McIntosh Red came along, or when they found you could make apples grow on the irrigated lands in the west. The Snow Apple is a little thing, not a spectacle in any sense and therefore unknown on the fruit stands. Like the Red Astrachan, it is an apple for eating around home—the kind a boy has in his pocket to stay him between meals.

The Snow Apple is a Fameuse, really. I suppose it used to be called a fah-murz, real French-like, but our Yankee forbears didn't go in for foreign stuff, and the name got changed to fay-muse. But mostly it is a Snow Apple, with little shreds of red running through the snow-white flesh, and besides having a flavor for eating at random, it makes a pie worth topping off with.

Then when winter came we really got pies. Then we had the Greenings, from up by the pasture bars, and the Baldwins. Also the King Tomkins, which is something like a Baldwin but better colored, and not bad to eat fresh. And the Northern Spies. The world doesn't have a finer apple than a Northern Spy—a spicy flavored booster that squirts juice all over the kitchen when you bite into one, and makes a pie all its own. It takes ten or fifteen years to bring a Spy tree into bearing, but it's worth every minute of it. By Christmas most of these winter apples are at their peak, and they come up from the cold-cellar without any of that store and storage flatness. After Christmas, and along by February and March the apple bins are beginning to empty, and Grandmother always moved along with the season to the ones that came mellow next. Some of these were without a name, as far as we knew, but they stayed hard until late, and had some flavor. We never had a Ben Davis on the farm, and I don't even intend to have his stepson—the disappointing Cortland. You can cut a Cortland in two for breakfast, and two days later it is still as white as when the knife passed through it. It makes a great thing for restaurants that like to cut up fruit salad for a couple of days at a time, but it won't pass muster when any other apple is handy as far as we care. The Ben Davis and Cortland are supposed to be nice for canning, but canned apples are unnecessary when anybody has a Fallawater tree.

The Fallawater is an apple specially designed by an apple-loving Providence for farmers who want to bridge the gap between the last of the apples and the first of August. The last I knew Farmington Fair was still offering a prize for the best plate of Fallawaters, but elsewhere in the pomological world I suppose they are gone and forgotten. They are a greenish yellow apple almost as big as a Twenty Ounce, and they not only keep right up to July the next year, but when you make a pie from one it tastes like an apple pie. You have to saw and split it, almost, and eating one from the hand is absurd. We had just the one tree, and it bore every other year. When Grandmother served her Fallawater pie in late May or early June, and said that this was the last of the Fallawaters, we resigned ourselves to an appleless meantime, and looked forward to August first.

Sometimes Grandmother fooled us. Sometimes she would find apples in the cellar after the apples were all gone. The old cellar was like that, and Grandfather always put in so many things he sometimes made a poor job of cataloguing them. He had the livestock in mind as much as his family, and even crooked apples got stored to give the hens a treat in cold weather. So Grandmother, looking for baking potatoes, might discover a bushel measure of hen apples that had been forgotten, and long after the last of the Fallawaters she would sit herself at the kitchen table and laboriously peel these apples with a pie in mind.

They would be wormy, crooked, full of rotten spots, blackended, and some of them would be all dried up with a green mold on them. She would pick them out,

‡129‡

cull them, pare them, and dissect them looking for enough for a pie. Sometimes they made a good pie, sometimes they didn't—but it was always welcome because we didn't expect it. To get that one little pie, Grandmother would turn out a couple of pails of pig material, and then Grandfather would take the pails down to the barn and announce gravely to his shoats, "Well, this is the last of the apples."

Pies! We had pies anyway, one kind or another. We had them even when we had other dessert—mostly because we never thought pies were dessert. Pies were part of the meal—good firm pies to settle and hold down the main nourishment. We knew Spring was with us when rhubarb pies were served, and we went along with the year to strawberry pies, raspberry pies, blueberry pies, wild raspberry pies, blackberry pies, peach pies, and sometimes Grandmother would treat us to a green tomato pie—really a wonderful concoction and well worth the time. She made currant pies, and wild gooseberry pies, and sometimes a carrot pie, which is maybe something like the South's sweet potato pie, which is supposed to be something like our punkin pie. Life, for Grandmother, was a succession of pie materials, and her reward was the love and gratitude of an admiring family. I think Grandmother felt she was well paid, and since those who praised her deserved her own best wishes, she could think of nothing more satisfactory than baking them another pie.

Grandmother never held her pies back. She kept them handy—not at the foot of the cellar stairs. Nobody ever laughed about her being mean with pies. Most of us remember her best coming jubilantly out of the pantry with a pie in each hand, and asking hopefully, "Who wants mince and who wants apple?"

PRESERVING the external home that Grandfather Jacob built is about the only condescension we made to the traditions. It's his house, all right, until you step inside, and we supposed we had the local monopoly on such a mingling of old and new until somebody said, "You got things Poothie Wortley never heard of." And because there may be some who never heard of Aunt Poothie Wortley, and because her story is left-handedly relevant, here is an account of her modernization of an ancient Maine farmhouse:

Back some years ago somebody offered Uncle Bill Wortley $2,500 for Broadloom Acres, and Uncle Bill laughed in his face. Today I imagine the place might bring five times that if the right person came along, but $2,500 was high tariff for a Maine farm then, and nobody made such offers for a place because he might get it. Broadloom Acres is Aunt Poothie's idea—it's the old Wortley Place to most of us—a beautiful stand of buildings right in the bend of Little River. The view across the meadows and up to the woodland behind is one that many women have wished they had out of their kitchen windows, and Auntie Poothie had it all to herself. Anybody would be glad to take a deed to the place at any proper figure, and the last thing anybody ever thought of was that Uncle Bill would sell it.

But without a word of warning, one day, he advertised an auction. Uncle Bill wasn't in any straits he hadn't been in right along, and he wasn't contemplating any change he'd discussed outside. It didn't make sense, but the auction bill included the "beautiful home estate of 260 acres more or less, free and clear of all incumbrances and available for immediate occupancy." The interest stirred up was great, and everybody planned to attend and see who got the place.

The truth was that Uncle Bill didn't contemplate making any change, and the auction was just a scheme he and Auntie Poothie rigged up out of the fertility of their respective minds. And they didn't have the faintest intention of selling the old home place, no matter how much they advertised it. What they did have in mind was perfectly sound, and made sense to them. It seems Auntie Poothie had said, one day, "Bill, I'm so sick and tired of this worn-out old furniture that I'd like to go on a shopping spree and fetch home a whole house-load of brand spanking new stuff nobody but me had ever sat on or slept in or et off or barked a shin on."

Uncle Bill, who never had any desire in the world greater than keeping Auntie Poothie happy, pointed out that, "This stuff you crab about is heirlooms, Poothie, it's stuff people would steal to get—why, Monkey-Ward would give you a whole bookful for that mahogany stand you start cabbages on in the front window."

Poothie said, "If they'd give me a chair I could sit in without making my legs drop off, I'd give them half

‡132‡

the mahogany we got. My idea of nothing at all is an antique that somebody's great-grandmother got the good out of before I was born."

So Poothie and Bill chewed it over, off and on by spells, and they decided to hold an auction and sell all the antiques in the house. The way antiques were bringing in money, they'd have more than enough to stock up on new things. And to draw a crowd they added the fine old farm itself. This was an outright promotional scheme, and they knew how to sell the place and keep it too.

They came up on our road and called on Cap'n Jed Blethen, and asked Cap'n Jed if he'd by-bid the farm when it was put up for sale. By-bidding was a common term in the old days, and probably still is if you aren't a gullible outsider bidding where you don't have any business. It simply meant that Cap'n Jed would appear to be a legitimate bidder, but would top any price offered by others, and eventually would buy the farm. After the auction he was to receive $10 for his trouble, and Uncle Bill and Aunt Poothie would go right on owning Broadloom Acres just as they always had. It was a deal, and the auction was advertised.

Nobody around here ever saw a crowd like it. The day was one hundred per cent, and nobody stayed away. City people came on the train and hired the livery stable to drive them out. Dinner was served on the premises, as scheduled, and the event was as much picnic as sale. Judge Cummings was the auctioneer, naturally, and for once he didn't have to hold a pitcher so the broken handle wouldn't show. The goods were top-notch, clean and bright. Nothing run in. The crowd was the best in his career, and he matched witticisms with them, and put the strangers in such a gay mood many of them bid fifty cents when they only meant a nickel, and they didn't care a bit.

The antiques were beautiful. The china took two hours and a half all alone, and neighbor women gasped at the prices paid for the bedroom furniture. Old braided carpets off the back shed floor went for as much as twenty-two dollars, and one woman wept for joy when she was permitted to pay thirty dollars for an old red meal chest with a wide pine cover. Uncle Jed, himself, had bought it once at an auction for thirty-five cents, and it was full of carpenter tools then. So they cleaned out Auntie Poothie's old junk from shed to parlor. She sat up on the porch with a grain bag full of bills, and making change out of a nail keg of silver, and dreaming great dreams about a furniture-buying bender in Boston, and Judge Cummings said, "And now we come to the farm itself, this magnificent estate with its incompare-able view and its rolling meadow fields in high state of cultivation, its ample pasturage and untouched woodland, bountiful supply of pure water, and how much am I offered?"

Then a funny thing happened. Nathan Tuttle yelled out, "Five hundred dollars!" and before he could get his mouth together again Artie Gifford called, "Five-fifty!" The way it came out, and the way an auction crowd works, every last person in the crowd jumped to the conclusion that Artie was a by-bidder, even to Nate, and after making this conclusion not one of them would make a further offer. Not even Cap'n Jed Blethen, because Cap'n Jed had taken this most inopportune moment to go down to the road and help a good-looking widow woman tie a whatnot on the back of her buggie, and he didn't know right then what was being sold next. Or care. So Judge Cummings bellowed and barked, and did his best, but not a face opened, and with the sweat standing out on his brow like the bore in the Petitcodiac River he knocked the farm down to Artie Gifford for five hundred fifty dollars, and Artie was astonished.

Uncle Bill went down to the road where Cap'n Jed was showing the widow woman how to make a double Blackwall hitch, and chided him for his inattention. After Cap'n Jed had regretfully taken his leave, Uncle Bill went back to the house, and the crowd had gone home. Auntie Poothie had Artie Gifford in the kitchen and was feeding him doughnuts and mince pie and brought up a pitcher of cider. She had told Artie the whole story, and Artie thought it was quite a joke. Artie said he didn't have five hundred and fifty dollars anyway, and wouldn't buy a farm with it if he had, but he just felt like bidding on something, and he thought it was safe to mention that amount on a farm that would bring at least $3,000 any day.

So they gave Artie the ten dollars they were going to pay Cap'n Jed, and Uncle Bill and Aunt Poothie still live at Broadloom Acres with a house full of Hollywood beds and comfortable chairs, and not an antique in sight. The kitchen is made of steel cabinets, and the dining-room set is aluminum, and Uncle Bill had the first electric blanket in town.

IT has seemed funny to a lot of people that my early experience with the horses around these parts left me perfectly willing to omit horses from my program. To those who just love to ride, and who prattle about dashing through the snow, and who get real horsie and go to horse shows and can quote blood lines, I gladly grant my share. I was not brought up to love horses. No doubt the horses I knew had something to do with this, because here and there this farm has had some nasty horses. It has also had some darling old plodders nobody could help loving, but life has demonstrated that a wheelbarrow, let alone a tractor, is likely to speed the harvest home.

But I don't think it was so much the horses that brought me up thus—it was the deadly, uninteresting times I used to have whenever one of them figured in my doings. Have you ever been out for a ride in your exuberant youth and had to sit still in the buggy seat while Grandfather conducted a dooryard call? A dooryard call was one of the most natural things in the world around here, and never a decent day went by but some-body stopped off in passing and conducted one. One that came to your dooryard wasn't bad, because being a child you could go off and hunt for hens' nests and pay no more attention. But one in which you did the call-ing, and you had to sit there while Grandfather ex-hausted the gamut of conversation, was sheer torture.

I remember one morning Grandfather had me help him find and catch the buck sheep, and after we caught him we were going up to Kettlebottom and swap him. It is good policy to swap bucks now and then, and get some new life into your sheep. It is sometimes hard to find a buck, but we made out, and it is easy to catch one. You just stand still, after you have found him, and he will come up and rout the puddings out of you with the top of his head. It doesn't take more than three or four of these experiences to teach you to duck at the crucial moment, and then you make a reach for the gentleman as he goes by. We had a lot of fun, and we trussed the buck up and threw him in the back of the buggy, and away we went.

A buck, trussed up in the back of a buggy, blats all the time, and as you proceed down the road a great many people perceive that you have a buck trussed up in the back of your buggy. This brings women to side doors, men to barn doors, children out to the side of the road, and it is pleasant driving along with so many interested folks to wave to. So we went, and then Grandfather decided to make a dooryard call on Neddie Plummer, who was also hard of hearing.

Blatting and whoaing we pulled up opposite the shed door, and Neddie came out glad to see us.

"Whoa! How goes the battle, Neddie?"

"Hello Thomas! What say?"

"I say, how goes the battle?"

"Fine, can't complain. How you feeling?"

"Baaaaa!"

"Firstrate."

"Baaaaa!"

"Mrs. Plummer keeping fit?"

"Been firstrate."

The horse was now having her attention attracted to a fly on her rump, a little south of due east, and right where her tail couldn't participate effectively. What the horse did was stand on her two front feet and wave the hind ones around in the air. Grandfather said, "Whoa!"

The buck sheep said, "Baaaaa!"

Neddie Plummer jumped back, and then he saw the fly and clapped it with his hand, which made the horse jump again, and Grandfather said, "Whoa, you, stand!"

"Potatoes all in?"

"What say?"

"I say, potatoes all in?"

"No—best part of them's in, though." This was accompanied by a grin, it was a bad year for rot, and probably Neddie wasn't going to put in the worst part of them.

"Baaaa!"

"Mine ain't too bad."

"Looks 's if that off hind shoe was loose."

"What say?"

"Baaaaa!"

"I say, looks 's if you got a shoe loose—here, up! Lift your foot up, lady."

"Whoa, you! What's the matter?"

"Looks like a loose shoe. Lift your foot! Whoa!"

"'Tain't loose is it?"

‡138‡

"I think it is."

"Didn't notice it was loose."

"Baaaa!"

"Seems to be loose now."

"What say?"

"I say it seems to be loose now."

"Didn't notice she favored it any."

"Better have it set."

"What say?"

"You better have it set."

"Baaaa!"

"Whoa, you stand still!"

Such was, as far as I know, a dooryard call. The trip to Kettlebottom included five or six of them, each of which resulted in the discovery the horse had a loose shoe, and also in Grandfather's acquiring in some fashion all the news. For anyone who kept saying "What say?" he heard more than I ever did, and when he talked about the price of oats he came away with details about all the family. All I did was sit there on the seat and wish I was back at the farm.

The riding along, itself, is another matter. That was fun, and Grandfather talked about everything a boy wanted a Grandfather to talk about. But on dooryard calls a boy had no acceptable part in the goings-on —he just sat there and wished he was back at the farm.

A call at which you stepped down and went into the house was likely to be more interesting, but that depended. I went once with Grandfather when he called on an aged and infirm lady he had known as a girl, who was now widowed and alone, and all wrapped up in her own woe. The house was one of those musty old places, and not a thing in it a boy could possibly be interested in. The old lady lived with her cats, and the cats lived with the old lady, and neither party was too neat about it. My job was to sit on a couch while Grandfather and his boyhood girl friend mutually commiserated each other on the failings of old age.

Her trouble seemed to be extremely anatomical, and she dwelt on the symptoms, cures, and manifestations at length and with candor. Grandfather, not hearing well, was obliged to inquire for repetitions, and I thought it was scandalous how these two old people gabbled on over physical functions that I had been taught to regard respectfully. Not all calls were like this, but too many of them were.

I will say that when people called on us and stepped down, at least they got something to eat. Grandmother's eye would catch the nose of a horse poking past the kitchen window, and she had decided what to serve before she found out who was behind the horse. "No, no —don't bother, don't put yourself out," was the customary response to the invitation to have a cup of tea and sugar cookies, or maybe some gingerbread and milk. "No trouble at all," was the proper reply. We children knew to the second how long we could stay out and play without missing a cookie.

Grandmother's alacrity with the tea pot reduced our dooryard calls and increased our step-down calls. But it usually took just as much time. Grandfather would get his foot up on the step of the buggy, defying the horse to start up and run him down, and he and the man would talk and talk. If the man had his wife with him, Grandmother would stand on the other side of the buggy at a discreet distance and talk and talk. One family with a little girl used to call on us that way, and the little girl would sit up between the older folks, half on one and half on the other, and would so much want to get down and play with us, but the rigorous rules of a dooryard call forbade this.

I am sure the horses didn't like them. They would never stand still, but kept prancing and swishing, and when you turned them toward the road again and touched them up they would be off like a shot, and more than one of them caught a hub on our mailbox post. This didn't hurt the mailbox post, and it didn't hurt the hub any, but it would set the whole buggy over about a foot with a jolt that was enjoyed best by youngsters who stood back in the yard and saw it. It was a unique way to speed the departing guest, and the horse whose haste occasioned it was usually the one to be most astonished at it.

This business of calling is not to be confused with visitors. Visitors usually spent the night and were most likely relatives. Either that, or they were the minister. As I recollect it, relatives and the minister were the only ones who got out of the "caller" class. My mature belief is that ministers made a racket of it, but I would hesitate to let one know I said so. With a rent-free parsonage any sensible man could make out in those days whether he got paid or not, and I guess it was as soon not as anything else. I do know that the occasional visits of the minister to our house produced him more swag than he could have bought wholesale on any salary, for he not only visited around to dinner, but he was given food to take away. At our house, the only restriction was that he had to be a good minister. Grandfather was discerning, and he could tell a sick hen when he saw one. He despised a sanctimonious preacher, but he welcomed one that could talk like a man. Grandmother was more inclined to respect the cloth for what it might be rather than what it was, but she was also practical enough to vote for a better parson if it seemed advisable to make a change.

I recognize now that the minister's visit was accorded more pomp than should accompany anything not patently divine, but things were different in those days, and it was fair play for the minister to pat little boys on the head and make complimentary remarks at their mother. The minister of my youth was a flattering old fuddy-dud, and he always ate too much. Modern ministers, around here at least, don't come to call the same way so are spared a comparison.

When he came we had a table cloth. Instead of Grandfather's short grace, which was said without announcement, we now had a formal invitation for the minister to invoke divine favor on our simple meal. It was pretty sticky. The minister, who didn't know we always ducked our heads before daring to touch anything, now warned us by something like, "And now if we all quietly bow our heads we shall have a few words of earnest supplication for our Heavenly Father." We youngsters usually looked with half open eyes at each other and giggled—something we never did when the minister wasn't there.

Another thing about the minister's visit that baffled me was the lack of anything to talk about. Ministers, apparently, didn't know about horses and potatoes, and bees and pine logs, and all the things we talked about with other people. They never spoke of those things, and nobody in our family ever brought such subjects up. We children were terribly disappointed—the minister's visit had been billed rather heavily, and from the preparations you'd think the family was in for a treat. But we learned it wasn't worth hanging around for, and except for the food we found other fields to cultivate.

Once Grandfather was shingling the barn, and my cousin Laura and I took much interest in it and gathered up countless shingle bolts and old shingles, and we imitated the job as best we could. One afternoon while the minister was holding forth in the parlor, and the older folks were all on their good behavior, Laura and I came in from our labors dirty and draggle-tailed, and were both excused for our appearance and introduced to the minister.

"Ah, such adorable little children," he said, making an of-such-is-the-kingdom gesture, and he said to us, "What have you lovely children been doing?"

Laura will hate me for saying it here, but it was she who told him. "We been shingling the backhouse," she said. Which we had, and we saw no harm in it, and I don't see any now. But Grandmother was dismayed and ashamed, and I think she never got over it. Grandfather, however, gave us both a nickel for next trip to town, and claimed it was because we picked up so many shingles and saved him the trouble.

In late years the automobile has widened the area of dooryard calls. People can come forty miles or more for one, and folks in the cities can get out for a breath of bucolic air and home again in time for supper. I don't know how the children would act if they still had to sit in the automobile during the call. But they don't. They swarm out of the car and up the side of the barn with absolute indifference to the purposes of barns, and a motorized dooryard call is likely to leave the farm folks glad they are soon gone.

Not always. Time and again we've had folks drive in and enjoyed every minute with them. But mostly that was after I inaugurated the custom of letting the buck sheep out Sundays, as I found that had an educational effect on city children who came with their parents to call.

Motorized dooryard calls usually include a walk about the gardens, and it distracted me to be telling about high-bush blueberries to interested parents, and out of the corner of my eye see their offspring taking the hayrack apart or pulling feathers out of a hen. It is all very well to insist that city children ought to be instructed in the purposes of domestic fowl, and that they should learn a thing or two about farm equipment. But it doesn't work, because city children see only vacation material in the country, and to some extent it is probably their parents' notion too. So a child who rides on the elevated and never touches the conductor's valve will arrive out on the farm and start up the milling machinery, un-wheel the hay rake, pull down the track-fork rope, let out the hens, throw stones at the ducks, and generally make an honest farmer pine for an alder switch and five minutes free time. With native Yankee shrewdness I reflected on this, and decided the automobile age needed something the horse and buggy dooryard visit got along without. I saw two main differences —in the horse days the child who was door-yarding knew better than to poke sticks at the cows, and he also stayed put and couldn't have done it anyway. The city visitor didn't know better, and he was allowed to run at large. ——— I immediately thought of two possible solutions. The first involved bees. At one time Grandfather used his hives of bees to keep school children from stealing apples on their way by. He set fifteen or twenty hives in a row around his Somerset tree by the road, and not a child dared run this gauntlet. The apples were saved, but another disaster struck. Bob Garfield was going by on the road one day with a load of logs, and he dropped one rein. He yelled at his team, but the team mistook his tone of voice and broke into a trot. Bob had nothing to do but haul on the one rein he had left, and this sent the horses off in a circle, and in executing this circle they ran over all the beehives. It was an awful mess, and everybody got stung, and some people said it served Grandfather right, denying little boys an apple or two off the ground.

The other possibility was the buck sheep, and I simply turned him loose one Sunday morning. He roamed around the dooryard looking for somebody to give him a chance, and as we didn't give him a chance he merely ate here and there and bided his time. And right after dinner a big new automobile drove into the yard and some friends of ours boiled out to make the modern version of a dooryard call. With them was little Eileen, a handsome child of about nine, who already knew far more than the combined faculties of the six leading universities, and was all set to dispose of the whole countryside with abandon and glee. I was thoroughly fair about it.

I took her to one side and I said, "Eileen, I think it would be just as well if you didn't go near any of the animals, because you might frighten them." Eileen looked at me with a grin. "Animals," I said, "Like that poor old sheep over there." Eileen looked at the sheep.

Then her folks joined me in a walk among the flowers, and down by the raspberries, and under the laden apple trees, and to the pasture-lane spring where we sipped the refreshing water, and then back along by the pond to watch the ducks. I contrived to stay so I could see Eileen, and the first thing she did was to pluck up some new carrots, about half a row of them, and hasten with them to the vicinity of my buck sheep where she proceeded to entice him with a carrot.

My buck sheep was a gentleman. He stepped up daintily and nibbled at the carrot, seeming most politely to thank her for it, and probably trying to apologize for putting her to this trouble. Eileen patted him on the head, and he liked it. Eileen no doubt was now assured this day was coming along as nicely as the last she had spent with us—a day it took me weeks to repair.

Then my buck sheep took up the cause of the aggrieved farmer, and undertook an educational campaign that I had heretofore been unable to start on my own. He provided nicely for the instruction I had so often wanted to impart to Eileen and her city-born hoodlums. My buck sheep made three distinct and separate retreats of about ten feet, alternated with rapid and purposeful advances, and he butted Eileen three sharp and effective butts on her chest, back and rump in such a way that he backed her up about thirty-five feet without giving her a chance to realize it, and Eileen found herself up on the shed roof where she got an ideal view of my buck sheep eating the rest of the carrots placidly and with gusto.

Eileen's mother and father were almost as astonished as Eileen. They gasped and shrieked and advanced to the rescue, but upon second thought they decided a buck sheep that would treat their daughter thus would probably make no bones about turning on them, and they turned to me pleadingly for assistance and succor. "It's just the buck sheep," I said, "He does that when he gets a chance. Now over here I've started a bed of asparagus, but I don't like the stuff and have wondered why . . ."

Eileen, of course, has since been here many times,

‡146‡

and has shown a great diligence in paying attention to what I say. By listening to me she has learned a great deal about the ways of country people. I was not at all embarrassed when she asked me later why I kept a buck sheep, and I simply said, "I use him to teach city girls that they don't know everything." Eileen thought that was a good answer, and so do I. The rest of the week I keep my buck sheep tied up, because while his head is woolly and it doesn't hurt too much when he hits you with it, it is still surprising when he does it, and I would rather be surprised in another way.

I was able to use a drake much the same way for a time, but I think the drake got tired of it and quit. He used to come running at us, and would reach out with his bill and pinch your ankles. I suspect this was a drake's idea of being a drake, and although he made a great to-do over it, he really couldn't hurt anybody. We found out the simplest solution was to keep on walking. He couldn't waddle fast enough to keep up, and although he quacked and flapped his wings it didn't amount to anything. But time and again he pulled this on dooryard visitors, and they were petrified. They'd stand on tiptoes and squeal, and not know enough to walk along. As long as they stood still he'd put on a real show.

There was one other way to stop him, but I didn't tell people either way. The other way was to stoop over and pick him up by the neck, cuddling him in your arms like a kitten, and he'd quack and make believe he loved you with abandoned zeal. So he treed a lot of dooryard visiting children for me, and was a valuable asset. He cornered children running the tie-up trough over, picking green melons, disturbing setting hens, playing in the grain chest, and all those other distracting stunts city children love to do around a farm. I'd hear some child squealing, and after an educational interlude during which no damage was done anybody, I'd go and pick the drake up by the neck.

One day my wife's mother went out to pick raspberries, and we told her if the drake bothered her just to keep on walking and pay no attention. But she went into a panic, sort of, when he came up, and forgot what I'd told her. So an hour or so later we found her standing on the chopping block. The door had been closed to, and we couldn't hear her yelling. She said it wasn't funny. A movement was started to have me fix the drake for eating, but right after that he stopped doing it, and although we had him a couple of years more he never treed anybody again.

But what I was coming at is the great amount of dooryard neighboring that goes on, and how it grew to be a large part of country living. In the old days you counted on folks going by to give you the news, and when you went out yourself you returned the favor. Through a boy's eyes, whether he sits in the seat and listens to the older folks talk, or whether he gets down and is treed by a duck, it isn't too fine a thing. But the older folks enjoy it one way or another, and anybody up here who builds a house has to allow a door-yard big enough for neighboring, and a kitchen window you can look out and see who's here. The buck sheep is not essential, but his educational advantages will justify one whether you like sheep or not.

THE parlor in our house was just as much a parlor as that in any old Maine home—hardly anybody ever used it. It was accoutred after the manner of the countryside, and had the black-walnut horse-hair sofa that to my own knowledge nobody ever sat down on. I never did, and I never saw anybody else. The room had the whatnot, a mahogany table, odd chairs, a store-boughten rug, and a great many other fixtures which were just as well destroyed by the fire. Our parlor wasn't even opened up for a funeral in my time, which is supposed to be the second function of a Maine parlor. The wedding, first function, came just once in the whole history of the house—when Grandfather came home from the wars and married Rebecca the school teacher.

As I cast back for something to say about the parlor, it seems to me the best day it ever had was when they fought the battle of Gettysburg in it.

The battle of Gettysburg is still a mighty subject in these parts, and the sheer arithmetic of the Maine boys who fought in it is something Maine has both cheered about and wept over. And it is no tall-tale that Grandfather himself started it. We sort of thought Grandfather's own story of that engagement was his privilege of embellishing a fact or two, and we let him go on all those years without raising any question. But we found out later he really did start the battle of Gettysburg, and the remaining members of the 16th Maine confirmed his remarks in every particular.

The way Grandfather used to tell it, with a couple of us on his knees, the North and the South were both trying to avoid a battle of Gettysburg. It wasn't a likely spot for a good tilt, and neither side had much to gain from trying to lick. But for some reason both armies were drawn up staring at each other, and Grandfather and his friends were among them.

Now Grandfather told this yarn, and as we heard it even as children we took it with a grain of salt, and as I have sometimes repeated it I found nobody is willing to believe it. Maybe I can get Gramp's own words down:

"So there was your Grampie sitting in the sun wishing he had an apple to eat, and up comes a big general on a white horse, and he dismounts and salutes, so, and says, 'Thomas! the prisoners need water. Form a guard and pick ten men to fill canteens.' You see, we had taken some prisoners, and they were all lined up in a place like a hen yard, and they hadn't had a drink all day. So I calls Frank and Dan and Jim and Artie, and we got some of the prisoners to gather up all the canteens in the prisoners' camp, and we started marching them down to the brook.

"This little brook ran through a patch of trees, and when we got down to it the water was tinklin' along and it was cool and nice. The prisoners filled all the canteens, and before we started back with the water somebody says 'Let's take a swim.' So the prisoners put their canteens on the ground, and we guards stuck our muskets against some trees, and quicker than scat we all off with our clothes and went to splashing in the brook. It felt good, and we had a nice time, but whilst I was ducking Dan I looked out the corner of my eye, and I saw one of them prisoners sneaking up out of the brook toward the guns. I let out a yell, and started after my own gun, and the rest of the prisoners and the rest of us down in the brook commenced batting each other around, and it didn't look good. But I got to my musket first, and I flung a ball at the prisoner, and he took to the bushes for keeps.

"Well, you know what happened—up on one side of us was the whole Union army just itching to have somebody start something, and down on the other side was the Confederates hoping to oblige them, and all either side needed was for somebody to take a shot at somebody else. When that gun of mine went off both sides thought it was the other side, and inside of five seconds the musket balls was ripping through those trees like hailstones, and I was so scared I got my pants on back to the front and when I couldn't run I thought I'd been wow-nded. Dan Small got into Frank's clothes and the two of them was standing there fighting over it and not paying any attention to the musket fire. I don't know what happened to the prisoners, but we laid in the woods until night and didn't gaze around much to see if the weather was on the make.

"After a while both sides stopped shooting into the woods, and began shooting at each other, and when it fell dark we crept out and found our regiment hard at it trying to stem the onrushing tide of battle. It went on three days, and was one of the most famous battles in history, and when it was over I tried to tell people I started it, and they been laughing at me ever since. But your Grandfather did start it, and while it was all a mistake, I claim he ought to get credit for it just the same."

Well, the thing varied somewhat from telling to telling, but it went about like that, and we children loved to hear him tell it, and never thought for a moment that history had dealt our own grandfather such a stellar role. But when I was in my 'teens the old parlor of the house was opened up, and Grandfather entertained the members of the 16th Maine Regimental Association. Naturally these associations have gone out of style, but in some places they still meet once a year in tribute to the soldiers who can't come any more. The soldiers used to come, wearing their Grand Army uniforms, and with them came their families and descendants. Except for Memorial Day, it got to be the only appearance Grand Army men made. It was really a reunion, and while grandchildren and aunts and all the others tried to amuse themselves and be quiet at the same time the old soldiers would commune and reminisce.

On this August afternoon quite a few of the soldiers came. Not only most of the local soldiers were in that regiment, but this was a good day and some from long distances had felt equal to the trip. I remember one old fellow, I think his name was Wardwell, who came from over to Gardiner, and as I remember it he either had a wheelchair with him, or they said he had to use one all the time at home. He was a fine-looking old soldier, and everybody was particularly glad to see him.

During the afternoon this soldier sat expectantly, and when he was called on for remarks he began to tell of some trying experience his regiment had been through, and a hush settled over the soldiers as they listened and reflected at the same time. He told of the advance they had made into enemy territory, of the courage of the men and the audacity of their leader. They had carried out their task with skill and speed, and then they found they had been hemmed in and retreat was impossible.

It was a wonderful story for a boy to hear. It was also a wonderful story for the old soldiers to live through again. They were leaning forward in their chairs, faces tense. The speaker mentioned some names—boys who hadn't come home and some who had. He told who the officers had been. He relived the whole skirmish and fought gallantly for every foot of ground.

Then he told how the men had sworn never to surrender their colors, and how they had squatted in the mud of the battle field in the dead of night, and had ripped Old Glory to tatters and shreds rather than let it fall into Southern hands. The tatters were distributed among the men, and the next day they were ready to be captured—each with a flake of his country's flag hidden somewhere inside his blue uniform.

It was, indeed, a grand story for a boy to hear. Then the old fellow reached inside his Grand Army suit, and fumbled for a minute, and brought out a torn piece of blue cloth, with part of a star in one corner, and he held it up and cried, "And here is the piece they gave to me!"

The old soldiers leaped to their feet and cheered, tears rolled down their cheeks like the ointment on Aaron, and there wasn't a dry eye in the house. But during that same afternoon some of the soldiers got to telling about that swimming party at Gettysburg, and those who had been on it related in detail everything that Grandfather had told us so many times. I was amazed to find the old cuss had been telling a straight story, and I'm afraid I still think, to this day, it would be a better story if it weren't so. Before they got through they'd re-fought the whole battle in our parlor, and while it was all most fine for a boy, there was one thing I've always been sorry I heard.

That was when Grandfather, talking with another soldier, said that on the second day of Gettysburg he had fired eighteen times—"and each time I saw my man." Somehow the Civil War had always been a joyous outing that Grandfather had been on in some lost age long before we children were heard of. There was no blood in his stories to us. It never occurred to us that quiet old Grandpop with his feet in the oven could have hurt anybody. He told me later that the fighting at Gettysburg, on Little Round Top, was done from behind a parapet, and it took so long to load the old muzzle-muskets that the troops participated in waves—one wave loading, another coming up to fire, a third firing, and the fourth retiring back to reload. After the first couple of volleys the whole battlefield was a cloud of smoke, and out of this smoke the advancing Confederates appeared like gray ghosts to attract the eye of the Yankee farmhands. Grandfather didn't like to remember that but perhaps more modern soldiers would like to know that a full day's firing at Gettysburg involved eighteen shots. And eighteen men.

True as that story turned out to be, Grandfather was not above embellishing his war stories, and could twist a cow's tale as well as the next one. These, he never expected anyone to believe. Such as the old one that a general rode up on a white horse—it was always a white horse in Grandfather's stories—and cried out, "Stop shooting, Thomas, you've killed enough." As far as I can learn every old soldier told that story, and it is possibly an index by which scholarly dissectors can isolate the virulent germ of Yankee humor. For my money it combines all seven types of humor in one, besides containing the salient properties of a perfectly intelligent and non-humorous remark. I think it is such an essay at humor that not above two or three differing types of humanity have ever tried anything like it, and it is all the more remarkable therefore that it had a tremendous vogue in this immediate vicinity. The success of the story, probably it would be a gag today, lay mostly in the fact that Grandfather told it chiefly so Grandmother would shush him. In this way it became a family by-word, and you won't be around our place long before somebody says, "stop shooting, you've killed enough!" with reference to some such ordinary work as shelling peas or paring apples. I leave further consideration to the professors.

Speaking of the parlor, its use for a wedding also involved Grandfather's war stories, and probably one of his best—the one how President Johnson postponed Thanksgiving just so Thomas could get home for a piece of Aunt Martha's punkin pie.

The evidence isn't wholly against this story, either, and the listener simply had to take it all and discount when necessary. Because President Johnson *did* postpone Thanksgiving, and Grandfather did get home in time to have not only a piece of punkin pie but a whole pie at that and a full meal besides. The way he used to tell it (and his feet in the same oven that baked the pie), he was at Appomattox in April, and shortly thereafter was in Washington, D. C., where they had a big parade and walked his feet off. They were still mourning pretty much for Lincoln, so the victory celebration was toned down, but they were holding a few private skirmishes about the city and Grandfather found out that Hannibal Hamlin was having a taffy-pull for Gens. Oliver Otis Howard and Joshu-way L. Chamberlain, and being as Grandfather and Joshua were woodpile cousins, Grandfather felt he would like to be present and pull for Joshua against the gentlemen from Penobscot and Kennebec. Grandfather had not seen the General in ten years, except in the heat of battle when neither had time to extend formal salutations, but ten years ago at a merchants' picnic at Kettlebottom Joshua had patted him on the head and remarked that he was shooting up like a weed.

So, Grandfather said, he stood among the mighty in the crystal ballroom and greeted this one and that one with enthusiasm and decorum, and had a nice time. Seeing him among such stalwart people it was only natural folks mistook Grandfather for a personage and a scholar, and many came up and grasped him warmly by the hand. So President Johnson, when he arrived, showed much interest, and asked Grandfather to come over to the White House while he was in town and see the new curtains in the front room and enjoy a good chat. He did, and President Johnson assigned Grandfather to a dangerous mission which was so secret Grandfather lived sixty-eight years afterward and never told anybody what it was. While he was on this mission his regiment was mustered out at the State Park in Augusta with the adjutant general on a white horse and the houses decked with flags.

Detained as he was, Grandfather complained to President Johnson that he wouldn't be able to get home

‡156‡

in time for Thanksgiving, whereupon President Johnson said, "Thomas, I had thought of that. When, in your declining years you sit with your feet in the oven and your grandchildren on your lap, tell them that once the President of the United States postponed Thanksgiving just for you! Go home, Thomas. to your well-earned repose, and I will issue a proclamation delaying Thanksgiving until you get there. Farewell!"

Grandfather never expected anybody to believe this, but I have looked it up and it is true that in 1865 Thanksgiving was held on the first Friday in December, whereas we have always had it on the last Thursday of November. But Uncle Timothy, who was a very small boy on that day, could remember it, and he said it was the best Thanksgiving we ever had. He said Aunt Martha baked a twelve-egg punkin pie in a bakersheet and Thomas ate every speck of it. Thomas got home on that Thanksgiving morning.

Uncle Timothy said the kitchen was full of women for three days mixing and fixing and baking. On Thanksgiving morning Uncle Timothy was sitting on the kitchen steps wishing he had a doughnut, and he looked up and saw Thomas striking up through the snow in the front field with his musket crooked under his arm. Uncle Timothy yelled, "Here he is! Tom's home!" and he said for fifteen minutes all he could see was women going by. They all kissed Thomas right down the line, even to Beth Coombs, the hired girl, and then Rebecca Foster climbed aboard of him again and never did let go. They were to be married in the front parlor the day he came home.

Aunt Martha, who was Grandfather Thomas' own mother and Uncle Timothy's, was "aunt" even to her own children, and she stood and looked at Thomas in a trance until all at once she said, "The pies!" and she ran into the kitchen to get the pies out of the oven. Thomas, Uncle Timothy said, went up to the kitchen door and stood there with his shoulder leaned against the jamb and smelled Thanksgiving morning with the tears streaming down his face.

Uncle Timothy always said the only thing he'd been able to smell all morning was doughnuts, but Grandfather used to tell us he could smell ten thousand separate and distinct smells. He used to try counting them off to us on his fingers. There could have been that many, according to the things they said about Aunt Martha, for when she made Thanksgiving dinner she wasn't wasting her time. This, being a special Thanksgiving for Thomas, was also special because the Fosters were all to be on hand and a family's reputation was at stake. It would also be Martha's last trip in command, because Rebecca Foster was coming to live. Mothers have to move down a notch in due time, and as the farm was Thomas' his wife would run the house. So Aunt Martha was right out straight.

She had five roosters roasting, and as Thomas watched they basted them, Rebecca and Beth Coombs stood on each side and held the pan two-thirds out of the oven while Aunt Martha reached in with a long-handled spoon. The roosters sizzled and spit like pitch in a pine knot, and steam rolled up to the ceiling, broke toward the walls and filled the kitchen with the balm of a thousand flowers.

Grandfather always told us about the roosters first. Then he spoke of the sage smell—from the stuffing in the roosters. It was potato-yeast bread a day too old to eat, crumbled and tossed with new onions, salted and peppered, shot through with beechnuts gathered on the first frost, everything held together with melted sweet butter, and then the sage. About that time they slapped the oven door shut, and the three women hung their pot-holders on the nail.

Then Aunt Martha made the rounds of the kettles on top of the stove. First was the onion kettle, because onions take longer to cook; then the turnips sliced thin, and the carrots, parsnips and squash. These kettles were grouped around the biggest one, the one for the bag pudding. It had to boil for four hours, and Jennie Starbird had come over from The Kingdom to tie the string. Nobody could tie pudding strings any better than Jennie. Too tight or too loose—the pudding wouldn't be right. Jennie did it just so, and it always came out like a great full moon and the cloth folded back in a puff of steam. Thomas could see the string sticking from under the "kivver," and it had a loop in it so Jennie could run through a pine stick and draw forth her pudding.

The second biggest kettle was for the potatoes. Grandfather always said potatoes and Rebecca were the only two things he couldn't find outside of Maine. Aunt Martha had gone down cellar herself to get them all the same size. They were rose potatoes, the kind with pink skins and pinkish edges after you peel them, and when the skins break in boiling the fluffy part sticks out all around them. Rebecca mashed the potatoes that day but she had to keep stirring them until Aunt Martha saw they were right and put in the cream and butter so Rebecca could stir some more. Aunt Martha said, "You might's well learn right now how Thomas likes his potatoes."

Then Grandfather used to say he looked out through into the pantry and saw all the things on the shelves.

Only he couldn't, because I've stood there and tried to see and the shelves were around the corner. He just knew what was there without seeing. For one thing, that punkin pie was there. For my part, and Uncle Timothy used to say the same thing, that pie was all I'd want coming home from the wars to make me happy, but Aunt Martha had been cooking for three days and it didn't take her all that time to make a pie. Besides all the pies she made she had the cake box full and the cooky jars. One thing Grandfather could have seen from the doorway was the doughnut crock with a wet dish-cloth under the cover so they wouldn't dry out. Uncle Timothy said he fretted over those doughnuts all morning, and that with so much pudding and pie he never did get to eat one. There were some left, but Aunt Martha wrapped them up and gave them to the minister to take home after the wedding.

Then Grandfather would mention all the other things he saw as he stood there in the doorway. He would run on about pickles until the juice ran down our chins—about all the kinds Aunt Martha had made herself and all the kinds the other women had brought. He told how one woman poured out a bowl of cranberry sauce, and another woman brought in a platter of cranberry jelly they'd been chilling in the shed. One woman worked at a bowl of butter making hard sauce for the pudding, and another stirred in the pitcher to make the soft sauce. Grandfather always took hard sauce. I always liked the soft, but Uncle Timothy used to take both at once.

Grandmother Rebecca used to hear him telling us these things, and she'd say that was the best Thanksgiving dinner she ever saw. But it couldn't have been any better than the ones she put on herself, that I can remember. I always used to feel badly because Uncle Timothy hadn't got to have a doughnut, but I found a person doesn't often need one by the time he's gone through a dinner like those. Grandmother Rebecca always used to pass around a plate of doughnuts last thing and say, "In honor of Timothy," and we'd all laugh and say no.

But that meal, I noticed, didn't make such an impression on Grandfather as the preparations for it. Because we never heard about how they sat down to table. After he'd tell what he saw from the doorway he'd go right on to the wedding. Uncle Timothy was able to dwell on the meal, but coming from him it didn't mean much because every time he ate he was at a banquet, and one time was as good as another.

The wedding didn't take long. Grandfather wore his uniform and Rebecca had her mother's dress. We children always thought Grandfather had whiskers and Rebecca gray hair, but later we saw the wedding picture —they were both around twenty and Grandfather was as smooth-faced as an egg. Grandmother Rebecca was pretty when she was an old lady, but in that picture she was so lovely she didn't look real. Grandfather used to try to tell us how lovely she was, standing with him in front of the parlor fireplace to be married, but he never finished that part of the story—he'd stop all at once and talk about something else.

Uncle Timothy said the minister had eaten too much, and his mince pie responded at the wrong time, and it was the most impolite wedding the town ever had. Rebecca's father went dead asleep and they had to wake him up to give the bride away. Uncle Timothy said nobody should ever plan a wedding on a full stomach. But later in the afternoon the dinner wore off and things perked up so they had a lively time of it before Grandfather and Grandmother got in the red pung and drove up to spend the night with the Newcombs at Peppermint Corner. They came back the next morning, and Rebecca took over, and Aunt Martha never bossed Thanksgiving again. She and Rebecca got along fine, because both of them were too fine to make anything of two women in the house.

So that took care of a wedding in the old house, and from all the reports it was as good as eight or ten ordinary ones, particularly where President Johnson set the date. If Grandfather had insisted Hannibal Hamlin and Joshua Chamberlain had come to the party, I might have doubted it, but he didn't, and it is also recorded history that in that year Thanksgiving was on that first Friday in December. Even if recorded history had made a mistake, there is one particle of evidence too convincing to ignore.

Because Uncle Timothy said that the whole day so unnerved Aunt Martha that she went to bed early because she was tired, and then she came right down again and said, "I forgot to put the beans to soak." She soaked an extra cup because Thomas and Rebecca would be on hand.

And if Great-grandmother soaked beans that night, you can bet your last dollar it was a Friday.

JUST up the road a piece there used to live an old fellow who was easily the biggest braggart in the world. The worst of it was, everything he bragged about doing, he'd done it. He'd come into the house and tell about some whopping great feat of strength and endurance, and no man living would believe a word of it. But the truth was that he had performed this feat with success, and never once in his lifetime did anybody ever catch him in a tall story.

Reuben Miller was his name, a medium-built old farmer with a gray beard down over his necktie, if he ever wore one. He was Grandfather's age, approximately, and had been just too young to get in the Civil War. Grandfather had been just old enough. Shortly after Grandfather got home again and was running the farm here, Reuben came down one day and asked permission to haul some logs out over our land. He had a considerable stand of big timber in back, and it would be easier to knock down the fence and bring the logs out over our land.

‡163‡

He came down to ask right after supper, in the cool of the evening, and he stayed to play a game of checkers with Grandfather. That was the first time these two ever played checkers, but the last time was about a week before Grandfather died—and never once in the sixty-odd years between the first and last did Reuben ever win a game. I don't think it was because Grandfather was a good player, because I used to win from him once in a while as a boy—I think it was a judgment of Providence, and the burden Reuben had to bear for being a braggart. There was one thing he couldn't boast about.

Well, the next morning he showed up at the crack of dawn with a big team of horses, and he went into those woods like a dog into a flock of grackles. He laid trees around without half trying, and performed each day as if no effort was required to do what will tire a whole crew of men. He rolled logs onto his rigging all by himself, and drew the chains taut and would come driving out of the woods standing on top the load with his feet braced apart and his team coming like the winner in the Circus Maximus. He'd yell and shout, and be off up the road to the mill as fast as his team would go. He logged off his whole piece in hardly any time at all, and then he would go visiting around and tell everybody how hard he worked and what mighty things he did.

He would tell about it while down here playing checkers, and everybody knew he was telling the absolute truth. Then he would lose every game of checkers he played with Grandfather, and would get up disgusted and go home.

There is no doubt in the world Grandfather's game of checkers spared us the shame of being second-raters.

We never produced a giant, and hardly anybody in our family ever went at work for work's sake. Grandfather was a leading exponent of the head-saves-hands movement, and he would sooner sit idle than tackle a stout job just for the sake of bragging that he'd done it. Grandfather would probably have languished for shame in the light of his neighbor's triumphs if Grandfather hadn't been so all-fired lucky at checkers.

As the years advanced Grandfather capitalized on his game by using it as a damper on Reuben. Long ago he had found that a licking at checkers took the talk out of Reuben, so when Grandfather noticed a case of bragging coming on, he'd hike up to Reuben's and have a go at the board. I remember once the thing worked, and it was perfectly clear what Grandfather had in mind. It had to do with our line fence.

Line fences are a mutual obligation—each farmer is obliged to stand half the fence. But long ago, when fences were first "viewed" by town officers appointed for that purpose, certain concessions were made to geography, and the division of obligations wasn't always to the split foot. Men whose land lay in fields had to bring their posts from some distance, but a man with woodland along the line cut his posts right there. So they figured out an even division, giving the man with handy posts more of the linear fence. In those days Grandfather's land had just been cut off, and Reuben's was wooded, so the fence viewers gave Grandfather a short distance up along a swamp, and told Reuben to do all the rest of it. This was a fair division, and is recognized even today.

But in a few years Reuben cut his land off, and Grandfather grew some hackmatacks and fir, and the original division was no longer fair. But neither of the two raised a complaint, and it came time to rebuild the fence. Grandfather went out and cut his posts, and stretched the wires, and worked for a week or more on his short section of the line.

Reuben, a good neighbor and eager to hold up his obligation, came down one morning about daybreak shortly after that, and he whaled into his end of the fence and worked all day at it with no quarter for himself. He cut posts, drove them into the ground, stretched wires, braced everything, and came down late in the evening—all done. He'd built his longer end of the fence in a single day. And Grandfather admitted it was built better than his own part, heavier posts, better bracings, tighter wires. All that remained was to have Reuben come around and brag about it.

So that next afternoon Grandfather hiked off up the road to Reuben's, and he said he didn't feel like working and would like to try out the checker board. He came home later, feeling very fine, and Reuben never said a word about how much fence he could build in a day.

This was all very well, but what I'm coming at is the picture I have in my mind of those two old fellows sitting by the window in the kitchen with the checker board on their knees. They were two of a kind, their beards the same cut, and almost of a size, although Reuben was bigger. It was usually a rainy day, and for years and years they had swapped rainy days with each other —down here, then up to Reuben's. They'd sit all afternoon without a word, except a brief post-mortem after each game when Grandfather would go back a few moves and show Reuben where he lost. But Reuben never learned—Grandfather said he was never more than a two-move player, he couldn't project the game ahead in his mind beyond two moves. Grandfather probably was a three-mover, and that was the difference. Because almost everybody else beat Grandfather any time he tried.

The checker board was, as far as I know, the only kind of organized diversion the old house ever knew. Playing-cards, which might have beguiled many a tedious evening, were still considered too likely to promote wickedness and sin. I can remember myself how cards were spoken of in the same way upright families still instruct the children about drinking and the advanced social crimes. Our later family didn't have anything against cards, and if anybody had thought of it we would have asked what's the difference between cribbage and checkers, but it was a cardless house from the early days just because it never got into the habit. It never got beyond the checker stage.

I'm glad it was before my time, but it is true that in the old days a family didn't feel it needed that kind of amusement. That doesn't mean farm children didn't have fun—it just means they had their fun in ways the modern toy-making trade would deplore. I've heard my father tell how he played on rainy afternoons in the upstairs of the old carriage shed, where Grandfather made his beehives. Grandfather had a table-saw with a fly-wheel and treadle on it, and he would rip out his pine boards and make his own beehives. He had one hundred or more hives sometimes, and it took a lot of foot-work to saw out the frames and boxes. My father would go up in that loft when it rained, and play house with the beehives. He'd set up whole streets of homes, with some hives for stores, schools and churches, and he'd carry on all the traffic and neighboring. Our lad has an electric train, and the difference is sixty years.

‡167‡

The house was not without books to read, because Grandmother was well-read and was a great exponent of reading aloud. The modern reader of books, I suppose, doesn't know too much about that kind of reading, which was really an influence on the writing of the day and would be something to touch upon lightly in the history of literature. In the old days nobody went into a secluded nook and curled up with a good book. The nearest to that was to sneak up in the haymow with a Nick Carter, which was risky because such retirement opened you to the criticism of shirking the work. Besides, Grandfather would commandeer the dime novel and read it to see if it was fit for you, and after he had read it he would declare it was not. In the old house a diligent student might read apart in the summer and during the day. But in the winter nothing was heated but the kitchen, and after dark nothing was lighted but the kitchen. The oil lamp on the oilcloth table supervised most of the reading our family did. Grandfather, of course, had his *National Tribune* and *The New England Homestead*. But that was not literature, even if they can be called amusement. In desperation the younger folks would sometimes spell out the articles in them, but not to improve themselves, only to pass the time. When it came to reading, it was done aloud about the table.

During the years, the family included every age and sort—from merest babes to bearded elders who were deaf. A story, for that audience, had to have everything. It couldn't spend too much time with the reverent and mature, it had to lapse at proper intervals to the gay and young. It had to have something for mother and something for the eight-year-old. So an evening now and then was spent with a book and it was taken slowly and with ample time between chapters for discussion. It was a leisurely kind of reading, and probably a good kind. Folks in our family who went through it seem to have come out with certain instruction in letters that younger folks marvel at. They also, of course, grew up without meeting a lot of the good and wonderful.

But the kitchen was not without its diversion, and those were the days a boy could be listening to *Treasure Island* and picking over beans at the same time. Our family was not exempt from the book salesmen, either, although Grandfather always paid cash down and haggled for a discount instead of paying the dollar a week for twenty years. Some of the sets of books were still mostly untouched when the house burned, and our loss included a photographic cyclopedia called the Wonder Library, about ten volumes, and *The Messages And Papers of the Presidents,* which didn't turn out to be very helpful and fortunately was not kept up to date. But not many books came our way, and any that did were welcome, no matter what they were about.

In the parlor we did have a stereoscope and a pasteboard box full of pictures. Niagara Falls in Winter was a lovely scene, and I'm blessed if I can remember any other single picture. But I saw them all—beauty spots of the world in sepia tones. We'd get dizzy looking through the thing because we didn't know how to focus it. We also had a picture history of the Civil War, and Grandfather was in one of the old Brady photographs of the Wilderness Campaign. It didn't look like him, because he was a young fellow. Our idea was that the Civil War was fought by bearded grandfathers, because that's what we saw in the Memorial Day parade, but in the picture history everybody except General Chamberlain was a young man, and even those with beards appeared to be boys. We used to get that old book out and look at it by the hour, over and over.

Other than that I don't remember ever hearing anybody in the family tell about recreation and amusement around the old house. They all tell about the fine times they used to have, and none of them seems to regret having the house in his memories of youth. It may be that newer generations don't know how to amuse themselves, and resort to mechanical and invented play. Or it may be that the older generations didn't know what fun was anyway, and so felt no loss.

I do know that I've watched a good many people play, and I don't think anybody today would get the enjoyment Grandfather got out of licking Reuben Miller at checkers. I think checkers is one of our poorer games, but we've got a checker board in the kitchen of the new house just for the tradition of the thing, and I tell my wife it's an object lesson to keep her from bragging.

THE governor of the State of Maine laid the corner stone of our new house. It was unrehearsed and unpremeditated, and because of the dearth of public building at that time it may well be the only edifice he succeeded in starting during his four admirable years in office. It was, and he knew it, a put-up job —but Horace Hildreth went to the same college I did, and his being governor didn't particularly stop him from being Horace Hildreth at the same time, and I had no particular misgivings about putting up a job on him.

It was the 29th of August, 1946, and we had succeeded in starting up the town's concrete mixer. The workmen had been busy for some time making the forms for the foundation, and by spells everybody had taken a whack at running the mixer. The town highway commissioner told us we could have it if we'd fix it up so it would run. He is a smart man, and he knew very well this device would save his budget the expense of a machinist, and we also knew that once we got it running it would be wise to finish the cement work before he thought up a town job somewhere that needed a mixer. So we had it running, and Merle Brown, the boss carpenter, commented that the occasion resembled the formal laying of a cornerstone. He said we ought to toss in a silver shilling for luck, or have somebody repeat the Gettysburg Address, or something, and just then they came running and told me the telephone wanted me.

It was Judge Jack, our local Republican shining star, who says he ran for the legislature, but walked for the senate. He was now lining up a hand-shaking committee to be present when Governor Hildreth arrived on his pre-election tour of the county. He wanted a few representative citizens to show their interest, and he wondered if I'd come right down to the village.

I may have sounded disrespectful, but all things are relative and I don't think any man would give up pouring the foundation for his new house to shake hands with a touring candidate. But it was not that I loved Caesar less. And the moment of indecision sprouted a crop. I said, "You bring Horace up here and we'll let him lay the cornerstone of my new house."

Some people may not know this, but touring candidates, if they be important enough, are usually at the mercy of the newspaper correspondents with them. The several reporters who had been assigned to Horace's tour that day were sweating out a most dreary forenoon. Nothing had happened. It looked like one of those days when politics would be lucky to hit a back page. So the newspaper reporters in Judge Jack's office let out a whoop of joy, and in about fifteen minutes the whole Republican Whirlwind Tour blew into our yard with flags flying and politicians jumping out of automobiles by tens and dozens. Among them was our friend Horace, looking fit and hopeful, and every inch a governor

‡172‡

amongst all the would-be county attorneys, sheriffs, probate judges, legislators, and bottle-washers in the entourage.

We have wondered ever since how it happened, but somehow the short notice was enough to alarm the countryside, and by the time the governor arrived our yard was full of neighbors. Horace himself commented we had more people there than he'd met in the village. They shook hands all the way around, and as a matter of straight politics it wasn't a bad campaign stunt.

We didn't have time to set up bleachers, but my wife did mix up some punch and break out a crock of doughnuts and some cookies. I grabbed up a steel cashbox and filled it with whatever odds and ends seemed most likely to suit a cornerstone—the morning newspaper, a picture of the family, a list of the workmen's names, and other things we have already forgotten. The last minute we took a "Hildreth for Governor" button off Horace's lapel, and then we locked the box. Horace leaned over the forms and set the box gently in the wet cement, we placed a marble slab against the face of the form so the place might be known, and while the photographers took pictures we pulled the slide on the cement mixer and buried the box for nobody knows how long. That is why Governor Hildreth had cement all up the side of his suit when he spoke later in Lewiston, and it is also why his tour made the front page of the *Journal* that evening. I like to think it is also why he was elected hands down the next week in the polling, and I suppose some day old men will relate how the laying of our cornerstone elected a governor.

Later on in the process of construction somebody wrote a letter to the Federal Housing Authority, which was currently alleviating the housing shortage by forbid-

‡173‡

ing anybody to build a house. If the foregoing sentence seems ambiguous, it is only because time has elapsed since 1946, and you who read don't remember our federal arrangements of that time. Posterity might like to know that in those days they held public examinations, in which the questions were like, "How much is two and two?", "What is the opposite of up?", and "What is coal used for?" Persons who flunked these examinations were put on the Federal Housing Authority and were told to alleviate the housing shortage by forbidding anybody to build houses. So somebody wrote them a letter, and they sent us a telegram saying we had to stop building. The matter didn't progress very far, what with one thing and another, and we kept on building—feeling even the penitentiary would be an improvement on a one-room log cabin with four people in it. But we did laugh to ourselves during the squabble, thinking how funny it would be to expose the Governor of Maine as the corner stone layer of an illegal house. We hope Governor Hildreth credits us with kindness in not blabbing about that to the Federal Housing folks.

There was one other brush with the officials. Our local town government appoints a building inspector, and we thoughtlessly treated him with utter disregard. The truth is that our town doesn't have any zoning laws, and doesn't have too sure a set of by-laws of any kind. It is mostly a town in which you can do anything, subject only to public criticism and civil recovery. But we do have a building inspector, and I told him one day to let me know when he wanted to inspect, and I'd fetch him up. I don't know what anyone does if the inspector condemns the work. In most places an inspector is supposed to collect some small favor before he passes you, and the job is worth buying. But up here I gather that the inspector can condemn you all he wants to, and all you do is go ahead just the same. I may be wrong, but as far as I know he always passes everybody. He passed us, and we had a nice visit. He revealed, during the visit, that he didn't think we had observed the amenities too well, because he hadn't had any official notice of our plans. This left me feeling badly, because I wanted him satisfied, but it also raised the question of how you become official over local building inspecting. I still don't know, but our lintel is clouded with the disturbing knowledge that we failed somehow to comply with local building regulations. If we could only get straightened out on this, we might find our corner stone was improperly laid, and all together we have unwittingly placed His Excellency, the Governor of the State of Maine, in double jeopardy.

The official building inspector, however, was a piker compared with Harry Reid. Harry is our town dentist, and he takes Wednesday afternoons away from his chair. During the construction of our house he used these afternoons to come up and inspect the progress, and after two or three weeks the men referred to him as the inspector. They began to look forward to his visits, and on Wednesday mornings they would clean up shavings and lay boards up in even piles. They even watched for him to come, and the first to see him would yell, "Inspector on the job!" and then they would all be working furiously and act very much surprised to see him. Harry had nothing whatever to do on his afternoon off except stand or sit around and wait for supper time, so he gave generously of his time and did a good job. The only trouble was that he never criticized anything, and never made any suggestions about the work. Even when the men turned to him to ask if he liked it thus, Harry evaded an outright opinion and contrived to find out first what the workman thought, or what the plans called for. With a good builder in charge, my notion is that Harry served on our house with every much effectiveness as the officials. And I know he did a lot more good, because he gave the men incentive to have something new finished by the next Wednesday afternoon, and I think it is a good thing for competent workmen to be inspected by somebody who just looks and never says aye, yes nor no. My own notion is that we'd have been much less successful if Harry hadn't tended out so faithfully, and that with the good start of a governor, the regular attendance of our "inspector" and the intentions we have of living here the house couldn't help but suit us.

WHEN building a house up in this part of the world, you have to take into account the fact that everybody goes to Topsham Fair. This means that the carpenters will not show up on that day, and no matter how important a piece of work is laid out, it will not be done until Topsham Fair has ended. The truth is I went myself. And we also have one brick set into the fireplace which does not match the other bricks, and it catches everybody's eye and they think we made a mistake. We didn't—that is the Topsham Fair brick, sort of, and it calls for a story. You even build things like Topsham Fair into a house when you live where we do.

When Great-grandfather first came up here he had a claim on about any land he wanted to include when he waved his arms and said, "This is mine." By the time other folks moved in to be neighbors, he had his desires fairly well established, and put some fences around what he finally decided to own. One of his earliest neighbors was a man named Sawyer, and Sawyer was very neat.

He felt he ought to have a farm with right-angle corners, and it irked him because his back line went off so-fashion along my great-grandfather's fence. What he needed was a back line parallel to the road, so one day he came over through the beech woods and asked Great-grandfather if he would sell ten acres in such-and-such a shape, so it would give Sawyer a straight back line.

Great-grandfather said yes, he would sell as much as Mr. Sawyer wanted at twenty dollars an acre. This was usury, extortion and highway robbery not only for days gone by, but even for now. But Great-grandfather had figured Mr. Sawyer out very well, and concluded Mr. Sawyer was neater than he was astute. He was right, and a few nights later Mr. Sawyer came over with ten golden double eagles in his pocket and claimed ten acres.

That was a lot of money then, and I'm not so sure it isn't something to be glad for today, and it was a long distance to anything like a bank, so Great-grandfather fixed himself up a place to hide it. When he had built his big house he had burned the bricks for the big chimney down in the clay run, making a frog pond that had since filled in again. It must have been a terrific chore —the chimney had eight fireplaces, each with its own flue, and the customary big fireplace and oven for the kitchen. Now, with two hundred dollars in gold in his hand, Great-grandfather went up into the open chamber and dug mortar away from one of the bricks until it came loose in his hand. In behind it he chiseled out a hole big enough to hold his gold, and then he fitted the brick back in again to hide the hole. He didn't tell anybody which brick it was, or even that it was a hole in the chimney he used, for long years. To wind up that part of the story—we think this brick is the one we have in our new fireplace. It looks like it, anyway, and we had to guess from the ten thousand bricks that lay collapsed in the cellar hole after the fire. At least my Great-grandfather burned this brick in his youth, and until somebody proves otherwise we're going to claim it is the one that covered his gold.

How long that two hundred dollars lasted we don't know, but it was a long time because they didn't spend much money in those days. When my grandfather was in his 'teens they still had some of it, and at fair time every year he'd tell about one double eagle that came his way.

That year Grandfather and Lonnie Coombs had planned to go to Topsham Fair, laying their plans as youngsters will well in advance. One day Grandfather asked if he could go, and Great-grandfather casually said yes—the way a father sometimes does with his mind on other things. Great-grandfather forgot—if he ever remembered at all. But not Grandfather, and when Topsham Fair day came Lonnie showed up at the crack of dawn, whistled under the window, and Grandfather came down from his bedroom. The two boys went to the barn and hitched the mare to a buggy and were soon ready to go. As they came up past the house and the buggy clattered on the pebbles in the yard, Great-grandfather stepped out of the back door and yelled, "Whoa!" The mare stopped in her tracks. Great-grandfather stood there tucking in his shirt, the rising sun making his gray beard pink. He blinked the sleep from his eyes and said, "Where're ye bound?"

My grandfather related that his heart fell a foot. His father's tone of voice indicated the trip was off—the trip he and Lonnie had been looking forward to all summer with every assurance they might go. It was clear now that Great-grandfather had never intended it.

"Why, Father," said Grandfather, "You told me I could go."

"Told you you could go where?"

"To Topsham Fair. Last summer, you said . . ."

Great-grandfather said, "Have you got any money?"

"No-o-o."

"Then wait a minute."

The boys sat in the buggy while Great-grandfather went back into the house, not knowing whether to take hope or remain despondent. Of course, Great-grandfather went up into the open chamber, drew out his loose brick, and fished out a gold piece. He brought down a double eagle, as golden as the new-risen sun, and he handed it to Grandfather.

Grandfather said he said, "Now, take this. Don't climb the fence, but buy you and Lonnie tickets. Be careful with it. Have a good time. Don't be extravagant and don't be mean—and bring back the change."

Grandfather told me the story a dozen times—every year when Topsham Fair time came. He'd stretch his toes in the oven, tilt back his chair, and chuckle. Then he'd repeat it, "Don't be extravagant and don't be mean —and bring back the change." But Grandfather would never tell me how much he spent and how much he brought back. Or if he spent any of it. But I got the idea he thought he did all right by his father, and he certainly conveyed that his father did all right by him. At least the incident gave our family an oft-repeated admonishment, and while we don't have any golden eagles these days we do have an old brick in our new fireplace, a crook in the line fence next to Sawyer's, and once a year Topsham Fair.

As our house was coming along, the men began to talk about Elmer Keith and Wilbur Taylor and their

‡180‡

steers. Our carpenters are not really carpenters, although they're better than most who are. They're all neighbors around here, and they came to work for me partly to get us a new house built, and partly to give them something to do for the winter between chores. So their interest in the steers was natural, and as Walter and Wilbur are neighbors, too, we all wondered amongst ourselves how the matter would turn out. How they would do, that is, at Topsham Fair.

I have a great admiration for oxen, but am not a steer farmer myself. My only experience with them was when I was a small boy and Grandfather let me team the gray Durhams home from the upper field. They were beautiful creatures, fat and sleek, every rippling fiber a powerhouse, and when they settled ahead into the yoke whatever was tied to the chain gave way and moved. The slow, deliberate, almost effortless movement of the team deceived me. I thought they were lazy, and supposed they couldn't move any faster if they wanted to. The careful training they had received while Grandfather walked ten thousand miles beside them made sense to his frequent remark that, "The gait of the oxen is the gait of the driver. They were slow because he had trained them to be slow—slow and powerful and methodical. But I didn't know that.

That day Grandfather gave in to my pleading and let me drive them back to the barn. The sidehill plow was tipped to drag behind them, and the truth is they'd have gone directly home without any guiding at all. Grandfather handed me the goadstick.

He made his own sticks. They were elm, which is tougher than a winter in Greenville, and into one end he would set a needle he swiped from the sewing-machine drawer. As far as Grandfather was concerned this needle was sheer ornamentation, and he put it in only because goadsticks from ancient times have always included a goad. He never used the prick and never touched the oxen with the stick when he drove. He'd trained them to respond to the spoken word, to a push or a pull with his hands, or to funny clucking noises. He used the rod a little at first, but never the brad, when the steers were young, but once the lessons were learned he carried the goadstick over his shoulder in a most formal posture, and relied altogether on gees, haws, whoa-heishes and assorted orders in ox-tongue. When he passed me the goadstick that day he said, "Now don't you touch them with it; you just walk along and they'll stop at the watering tub." Grandfather wandered off to look at a cherry tree, and I dallied along up the lane with the oxen.

They moved too slowly for me, of course, so I looked to see where Grandfather was, and then I reached over important-like and bradded the off-ox gently and said gee at the same time and made believe I was an old farmer hauling off rocks. I didn't make believe long, though, because nothing like that had ever happened to the off-ox before and the team came to life and sprinted like two greyhounds off across the fields, right past the buildings, and on up the road towards Baffin Land. The plow was bouncing along behind them ten feet in the air, and I was not only amazed but told Grandfather I didn't have any idea what might have happened. Grandfather said maybe I didn't, but he did, and he was gone two hours before he brought the oxen back into the yard and told me I ought to be ashamed of myself.

I have never teamed oxen since, but I like to watch the other fellows do it at the fairs, and Elmer Keith and Wilbur Taylor do it as well as anybody around here.

‡182‡

So when Topsham Fair time came I went down with the rest of the crew on the house and watched the contest.

The contest itself is nothing to the getting ready. I called up Elmer Keith the night before to ask what time he showed, and his wife said he was out to the barn putting fingernail polish on the steers' horns. That gives you an idea. They primp them and curl them, and spend all summer insulting the owners of other steers, and go out every evening about sun-down to exercise the yoke and give everybody a chance to see they mean business. Elmer lets it be known that Wilbur's cattle couldn't pull a cap off a little boy's head, and Wilbur retorts by making elaborate inquiry as to how Elmer's "calves" are coming along and if he's weaned them yet. This goes on until all the neighbors have decided which yoke they'll back, and anybody who doesn't live around here would think a bloody civil war was about to break out over whose steers can pull the biggest load.

That's the way they settle it. At the fair they load a stone drag, and the yoke that can pull it the greatest distance in a given time gets a blue ribbon which is attached at once to the horns of the nigh ox and is more highly regarded by both ox and driver than all the gold in Fort Knox.

I hadn't seen either yoke that fall, but enjoyed all the sideplay from the carpenters, and had decided Elmer's ought to win. My reason was solely because of the hearse. Elmer trained his steers by hooking them to the body of Fred Crossman's old horse-drawn hearse. Without wheels on it the thing dragged heavily, and I figured anybody who could think up a use for an old hearse deserved to win.

So the day came, and there wasn't a nail driven in any part of the house, and everybody from around here was down at Topsham Fair leaning over the wire fence to see Elmer and Wilbur fight it out. The trial itself was a little irregular, since Wilbur fell down a flight of stairs that morning and couldn't very well drive steers from his bed of pain. His steers were there, smooth and sleek and pretty, but Wilbur sent regrets. Elmer went out with his steers and hooked into the stoneboat, and hauled it up and down the arena just for the formality, and they gave him a blue ribbon. Everybody was disappointed, including Elmer, and the judges were just about to start another class to pulling when Elmer came in driving Wilbur's team. The judges announced that Elmer Keith, driving Wilbur Taylor's steers, would now try to beat his own yoke. The cheer that went up was something I'm glad I heard, and people came running from all over the fair grounds to see what was going on.

It was quite a contest. Elmer got Wilbur's steers off to a good start, and then the stoneboat dropped into a hollow spot and seemed to get stuck. Wilbur's oxen went down on their knees, and Elmer had quite a time keeping them headed right. He geed them around for a slant-wise pull, and made them rest. The stop-watch ticked away, but Elmer held the goadstick across their noses and made them wait. When he thought they were quieted he brought them up tight on the chain, and dancing ahead of them with his hands on their horns he walked them the whole length of the arena, turned them neatly at the fence, and walked them back again. The stoneboat was smoking on the ground, and when he came up toward the place his own team had finished he walked them right on by it. So he took the blue ribbon off his nigh ox's horn and hung it on Wilbur's ox, and collected second prize and went home. "I'm so good I can even beat myself," he said. Wilbur said, "It just shows the right man can win no matter what he's driving." And all the carpenters said, when they came to work the next morning, it was the best pulling they'd ever seen.

In order to quote, "Don't be extravagant and don't be mean," I had the lad with me at Topsham Fair, and after the pulling contest we toured the grounds. A youngster growing up on this old farm has to make the rounds so he'll know what his ancestors did. I took him up in the big hall and showed him where his great-grandfather used to have an exhibit every year, with all kinds of garden stuff with blue ribbons on them, and always a hive of bees in a big wire cage. He used to sell slices of comb honey for ten cents, and the little girls of the family were allowed to go down with him to wash the dishes. Sanitation laws probably would have put him out of business in time, as the dishes were sometimes used and reused when business was brisk, and the girls kept washing four or five over and over to make customers think everybody had a clean one. Grandfather was a good businessman, and in this way he got over a dollar for a pound of honey when the going price was 20¢. He also took orders, and was able to spend a whole day making deliveries around the countryside. The bees flew around in the cage and attracted attention, and he had a good thing until one year his bees had a bad year and he didn't go. The next year he couldn't have his old booth back, so he quit.

The lad didn't seem to attach so much to this notable matter as I did. We wandered off down the midway and certainly did have a good time. Prices had gone up since I was a lad at Topsham Fair, and I concluded what this country needs now is a good five cent anything. Hot dogs were retailing at twenty cents, the same price as a ride on the merry-go-round, and you couldn't touch a jot of ice cream for less than a dime. Balloons had gone up to thirty-five cents, and the teeniest smidgin of solid gold, fashioned into a dainty pin with Mother engraved on it, set the lad back a whole half-dollar, and it was partly green before we got home.

Except for the price, of course, Topsham Fair was just the same as always. We used to ride at five cents a time, six for a quarter, and hot dogs were a nickel straight. Spun sugar doesn't cost any more than it used to, but you don't get so much on the paper. I explained to the lad that spun sugar is a fair-time phenomenon. Grandfather, who used to look around behind at any profitable venture, once said that selling spun sugar seemed to him a life of joy and bliss, inasmuch as the man poured in a spoonful of granulated sugar and made $482 from it. The lad decided spun sugar should be followed by a cinnamon apple on a stick, a bag of peanuts, a cooling beaker of sweet cider, some salt-water taffy, a second hot dog, a bag of caramel corn, a popsicle, ice cream on a stick dipped in chocolate, and a ride on the ferris wheel. His mother spoke unkindly because he ate sparingly at supper.

We pitched rings at ten dollars' worth of one dollar watches and won a beautiful banner which reads "Swing It, Babe!" We shot cork stoppers at big boxes of ginger snaps and won a lovely button which says, "I'm No Angel." We also won a lead boxing-glove for a watch charm, a little whistle which I buried the next morning, a plaster-of-Paris polar bear, and a Hawaiian ornament to go around the neck which I can't spell. We would have had a nice cotton all-wool blanket, but the man guessed his weight right on the nose, and that was a quarter lost. The man would have been wrong, but he knew that little boys at the fair are full of goodies.

The horse trotting caught his fancy and we had to go and look over the fence. I tried to explain why it wasn't a good idea to go up and sit in the grandstand, what with the modern degeneration of the sport of kings. Our horse trots have turned into a glorified pari-mutuel, and they aren't too much fun. We stood by the back stretch and saw one heat go by. The horses were trying pretty hard, but five drivers were pulling back on the reins so the sixth one could catch up, and the sixth one was pulling back so he wouldn't. I pointed out that the grandstand was on the wrong side of the track if anybody wanted to further public knowledge, but probably the folks wouldn't believe it anyway, and we went and had another hot dog and some more cider, and tossed rings until we won a handsome police badge and a celluloid stickpin which fortunately was lost before we got home.

We took a turn around the animal exhibits, and looked at the big punkins, and found that Sagadahoc Grange had won first prize again all right, with some of Mummie's double-knit mittens right in the middle of the exhibit, and I said, 'Would you like another go at the refreshments?"

The lad said "No" with extreme thoughtfulness, and I knew it was all right now to suggest going home. We picked up some balloons on a stick for a couple of the neighbor children who didn't get to go, and worked toward the gate. His hand was very sticky, and he had mustard and sugar and cinnamon apple and chocolate smeared on his face. "That's it for this year," I said, and he said, "Don't people have good times at fairs?"

I said, "Yes, they most certainly do, and next year it's your mother's turn to take you."

‡187‡

ONE time old Horace Jordan drove into our yard with a heifer tied to the tailgate of his express wagon, and he proposed to Grandfather that it might be a propitious day for the two of them to trade something. Grandfather said it was indeed a fine day, and he couldn't think of a thing he'd rather do than trade something for something else, but that as he reflected on his present stock of assets, it was growing increasingly clear to him that of all the things he didn't need right now a heifer was the outstanding non-essential.

Horace expressed amazement at this situation, and stated with finality that if Grandfather suspected in the least that the heifer was for sale or for trade, he had erred magnificently, since this heifer was one he wouldn't part with, b'God, for all the stock, goods, chattels, and intangible property on our farm.

Now that the two of them had settled definitely on the subject of their present trading, they began to talk about a number of non-related subjects, such as the weather, the price of loose hay, the news from the state legislature, and what Harry Loomis was going to do with ten acres of white turnips. Harry, that year, had decided to take a chance on rutabagas, and got white turnip seed by mistake, and was currently suing the seed company. He eventually lost the suit, but he still had ten acres of white turnips, and everybody was interested.

Grandfather and Horace Jordan traded each other all the time, and it was never many days on end that Horace didn't come into the yard with something he thought might tempt Grandfather into a rash moment. Grandfather was tempted many times, but he also tempted Horace now and then, and the two of them were bosom enemies and wary friends.

Once in Town Meeting the incumbent tax collector, feeling he had the job sewed up, presented the suggestion that his commission be increased. He was getting three-quarters of a percent on collections, and he felt he ought to get a full percent. Horace, who had the world's best knowledge of goods, markets, and rates, was furious at this open raid on the community treasury, and he arose with some heat and protested it was too much. He shouted, "I'll collect the taxes, b'God, for half a percent and be glad to do it."

Horace wasn't a candidate, he was using himself as an argument, feeling this remark would shame the collector into keeping his old rate. But Grandfather jumped up and nominated Horace for tax collector, and he was elected hands down. Horace made out he was mad, but when the tax bills came out he put them in a wallet and began making the rounds for his half of one percent. A trader by nature, blood, habit, instinct and profession, Horace was delighted to have some excuse to visit every home in town. Business was good, and by devious dickers all up and down the roads he was able to parlay his half of one percent into what must have been the best year's pay any Maine tax collector ever got. Horace used to say, "I wouldn't cheat you Thomas, you're the man got me this job, b'God, and I'm grateful." Then he would cheat Grandfather, and pretty soon Grandfather would cheat him back.

On this morning, when Horace drove in with the heifer, Grandfather exhausted his conversational diversions, and then rashly offered a flat ten dollars for her. Horace was aghast at such insulting comments, and stormed and fumed around the dooryard, and repeated his flat statement that the heifer was not for sale. He pointed out her fine lines, and related her lineage, and said he was going to raise her up and sell her for dairy purposes just as soon as he could find a young, promising farmer who deserved some assistance on his way up —such a one as would appreciate good breeding. He mentioned fifteen dollars as the lowest sum he could possibly consider, and that was only because he and Thomas were long friends.

Thomas still said ten dollars, and after some more storming Horace swung out around the woodpile and clipped his horse up the road with the heifer trotting along behind.

Grandfather made a mistake that day. He thought he was going to get the heifer for ten dollars. He thought Horace was going off up the road in a mere gesture, and that Horace expected Grandfather to shout after him to come back and he'd give fifteen. Thinking thus, Grandfather expected that Horace would get out of sight and when he saw his ruse hadn't worked he would come back and claim the ten dollars. But Grandfather was mistaken. Horace didn't turn around.

‡190‡

Acting under his illusion, Grandfather thought he would spare Horace the trip back. So he scouted through the bushes up along the road, keeping out of sight and abreast of Horace. The instant Horace showed signs of turning the horse, he would betray himself, and at that time it would be safe for Grandfather to step out of the bushes and lead the heifer home. But Horace didn't turn around, he kept right on going, and Grandfather chased through the bushes away up to the schoolhouse. That's as far as he went, and after a while he crept out of the bushes and looked up the road so he could see Horace and the heifer disappearing over the brow of the next rise, and then he walked home in the road and presumably wondered at just which point the dicker had failed.

The more he thought of it, the more he liked the looks of the heifer, so later in the afternoon he hitched up his horse and drove up to Horace's and reopened negotiations, and finally brought her home for ten dollars and three baby pigs. The next day, when Horace came for the three baby pigs, Grandfather pointed out to him the six other baby pigs in that litter, as well as the brood sow who nursed them and so life went and so Horace came and went, and it was always exciting when the old fellow drove into our yard with a dicker in mind.

Horace was not the only trader who came. But Horace must not be confused with peddlers, who came also. Peddlers were those who had a route, or came on stated days, or brought a particular kind of trading material, such as the fishman. Horace bought as well as sold, he took as well as put out, and he didn't care what commodity was called to his attention so long as it seemed to him helpful in his affairs at another home.

The bull he bought might be sold to a farmer for cash, it might be swapped off for hay and potatoes, or it might be slaughtered and would come around again as fresh beef. Horace was an old trader, and they don't breed them anymore.

Another trader who came was little Moses Epstein, who showed up here one morning when Grandfather was still a young man. He had a pack on his back, and hadn't been long in this land. He brought out his shoelaces, spools of thread, papers of pins, and conducted something this farm had waited a long time to see—a trade without conversation. Moses had the prices written on his goods, and he pointed at them. There was no opportunity to dicker. Moses had one price and was stuck with it. Grandfather shrugged his shoulders and went back to Horace Jordan and his other cronies. But in a week or so Moses was back—his pack bigger this time because he had more items.

Moses was a little fellow, with the meekness and shyness that went best with his latter-day intrusion into a trader's paradise. His scrubby beard was never any longer or any shorter, but each trip his pack got bigger. It was an odds and ends assortment of things every home needs, but none of them so big he couldn't get a good supply in his pack along with everything else. And with each trip he got a little more talkative, until there came a time he was able to carry on a decent conversation. Moses, of course, was just as much a trader as any of the others who came, but nobody thought of him as such, and he was a familiar sight along our dusty old roads for a long time before anybody tumbled that Moses was cutting in on a traditional Yankee territory.

The younger folks around here never heard of Moses, but I can remember the older folks tell of him.

‡192‡

They all liked him. He never cheated anybody, and it was well known that if Moses told you so, you could believe it. That was definitely something new in the local trading technique, because when our old timers tell you white is white, you can almost bet it's black that day. Probably it was his disarming friendliness. Coming around on his first trip without knowing a word of English made everybody take notice, and made most everybody curious. His second trip was all the easier. And it got so everybody was glad to see his grinning face, and Grandmother always cleared the table off quickly so he could spread out the things in his pack and state his case.

Then one day Moses came with a horse and an express wagon—a familiar old yellow horse and a familiar old once-blue wagon. It was Horace Jordan's rigging. Moses had dickered with Horace, and as far as I know the details of that trade went to the grave with both of them. Grandfather tried to pump them both, but he never got a word. Moses had Horace's rigging, and Horace came around a day or so later with another horse and wagon, and although men would have paid dollars to know, nobody ever did.

This time Moses was loaded for fair. He had ginghams and percales, lace curtains, and more things than anyone would believe a single wagon could carry. It was definitely a woman's assortment, and for many years that's the way it was—Moses came and beguiled the women into purchases, and Horace came and tricked the men into swaps, and these were our two outstanding traders.

Moses had a number of horses and each time a bigger wagon, and finally he stopped coming and Grandfather found he had opened a store at the Falls. Grandfather went in and shook hands with him, and Moses

‡193‡

showed him around. He had a better stock than the town had ever seen before—still stuff for the women. He gave Grandfather some little favor to take home to Grandmother, and after that every trip to town called for a visit to Moses' store. He sold that after quite a number of years and moved on. Wes Bradbury came home from a trip one time and said he saw Moses in a city somewhere, I forget where, and he had a store as big as two of our high schools, loaded to the scafflings with dry goods and clothing. He said Moses remembered him, and asked for all the people for miles around, one after the other, going from house to house the way he had covered his route. And one time when we had a bad fire in the village, and a lot of people took quite a browsing, old Bob-tail Blatchford, the lawyer, went around giving money away as free as water, and he put people back on their feet again. Nobody but Blatchford ever knew, and he didn't say, but a lot of people suspected it was really from Moses Epstein, partly because he was the only person anybody could think of who might have a reason for being nice to folks around here.

When the house burned we had, in one of the upstairs closets, some old curtains and table runners Grandmother had bought from Moses. And goodness only knows how many mowing machine parts, hand tools, sled irons and sundries laid around the barns and sheds —mementoes of old Horace and his sallies at Grandfather. It was years and years since either of them had set foot in our dooryard, but they were far from forgotten.

MY wife tried to telephone to Bettsy Savell one morning, the way women help each other with their housework, and she got plugged in on a busy line. The way our telephone system has been working up here lately she figured she was lucky to get anybody, so she listened and heard one of the women on the line say, "What do you think of the new house?"

The other woman said, "Ain't it awful? It looks just like a big fort. I wonder, while they was at it, why they didn't make themselves a nice, modern bungalow." The other woman said, "I know it, some people are awful foolish when they come to build." My wife claims she hung up after that and didn't hear any more, which may or may not be authentic reporting, but this seemed to be the way two of our neighbors felt about our efforts to rebuild an ancient landmark.

Time and again, out through the country, fires have destroyed the old homes, usually because the chimney has developed a flaw, and you always hear somebody say, "It's a shame to see these old places go, they never get built up again." This is mostly true. Either the cellar hole is left to grow up to alders, and the farmer goes out of business, or he quickly throws together a new house that is neither a credit to himself nor an improvement on the scenery. The early pioneers made big homes, and probably developed in their descendants the notion that a big home is a liability. Farmers, too, generally build their own places, and their knowledge of construction isn't equal even to the modest houses they start. Having been burned out, they are in a hurry to finish a new place before snow flies again, and it is altogether likely that the amount of building done by cold weather is all the work the house will ever get. Our old house was the oldest one on the road, the biggest one, and no doubt was the best built one considering the construction knowledge of the late 1700's. It did look just like a big fork, and when viewed architecturally it was neither adorned nor beautified, and to my mind was far more sincerely pretty than the ginger-breaded and bow-windowed contraptions of the nineteenth century. It had a hip roof, and you can't be much else except practical when you have a hip roof.

Looking like a fort has a geometrical value. The wall and roof area gives you the greatest inside measurements for your money, makes for direct and easy building in all dimensions, and allows unlimited adjustment of various directions to give any kind of a room arrangement you desire. And as we very quickly discovered when we began drawing pictures of what we thought we'd like, the fort-like exterior is no hindrance to a pleasant inside. So we rebuilt the old farm house just as Great-grandfather had laid it up so many years before —the six-over-six windows, the fanned front door, the red-painted clapboards. And we were pleased when the older folks of the neighborhood came up with the comment, "Looks just like the old house!" The older folks seemed pleased at this, and felt an old friend had come home again. We were also pleased when younger people, some who couldn't remember the old house, said, "Looks as if it had always set there, don't look like a new house at all." It's on the old foundation, it has the same dimensions, the same trees around the dooryard, and the hip roof with the square central chimney are just as they were. It ought to look like the old house, and it ought to look as if it belonged there—even if it does look like a fort.

After the housewarming, when all our neighbors came to see, we didn't happen to get plugged in on a busy line, and we didn't hear what the two women thought of the inside of the fort. Because our new home isn't much like the old one inside, and the difference is exactly the difference of 150 years. In gadgets alone, we put Great-grandfather's house so far ahead of Great-grandmother's time that she would probably have fainted at the extravagance. We found out what had been going on in the world in our log-cabin meantime, and were astonished ourselves at the things Merle, our boss carpenter, kept bringing around.

We first became gadget minded, really, when we saw a wire sticking out of a hole in the front-hall wall. The electrician told us it was for the door chimes, and we laughed. I said, "Who ever heard of a set of chimes in a Maine farmhouse?" He seemed put out a little, and said they were quite a thing, and there were people who weren't so backward but what they liked them. He said, "They ding once for the front door, and twice for the back." I said, "Anybody comes to a front door around here ought to get more than one ding for his trouble."

On the old house the front door didn't have any hinges on it in late years, and was nailed shut. I don't suppose anybody ever came to it. If anybody did, he banged for a while and then went around to the back door like a human being. He didn't have to ring a bell, because there wasn't any bell, and he didn't have to knock because the back door was always open in the summer, and everybody in miles around knew it was never locked in the winter. Besides, somebody was always standing by the kitchen sink window washing dishes, and before you could knock whoever was washing dishes saw you and yelled to come in. The whole idea of door warnings arises from congested areas, where visitors need to be examined before entering. Around here we assume that anybody who wants to come in is going to come through a door, and it will hasten them if the door be open, and it will spare us the trouble of going out through the summer kitchen to open it. We have always felt the arrival of a visitor is a desired novelty, and should be treated with respect and hospitality. It may seem hard for some people to believe, but the old farmhouse used to welcome peddlers and tramps with just as much of an open door as we used for the family itself. So we weren't altogether coy in laughing at the idea of chimes, even if it was disrespectful of modern invention.

But gadget follows gadget hard upon, and before we got the chimes set up Merle came around with something even newer. It is a kitchen clock that tells the time with unerring electric impulses, and it chimes for the doors as well. Once for the back and twice for the front. This seems much more practical. Chimes just stand and wait, but keeping time will give them something to do between visitors.

Merle isn't exactly like some builders in this world, and it was characteristic Yankee spirit that prompted him to advise us on all our gadget needs. He knew we didn't know about such things, and he assumed we would want the best and latest, so he frequently installed wonderful innovations without taking the time to speak about them. One day he put an odor eradicator in the kitchen.

Sweet and pure, our kitchen is never going to smell of frying doughnuts and boiling turnips. An electric fan will yank all such time-honored smells out through a grill in the clapboards, and even the wet wool socks drying on the oven door will give off homely scents that will pass by on the other side. A year ago I might have thought this was too much niceness, and would have argued hotly that a kitchen that didn't smell of boiled onions and salt pork scraps couldn't possibly be accounted a number-one kitchen. But as gadget grew on gadget I am now devoted to the successful marriage of sentiment and utility—I have my old great-grandfather's house on the outside, we have my wife's modern home on the inside, and harmony prevails. We can have our cakes, but we can't smell them too.

Merle also brought around an electric heater with a fan in it, which he set in the bathroom wall. He said we could turn it on to pep up the temperature when fallish mornings sneaked up on us, or we could use it to dry ourselves on and save towels. He said it was the same thing they have in Radio City and very nice. So we gadgeted that room.

We also ran an extra faucet into the kitchen sink, and we have a sign on it that says, "Spring Water." You can do silly things like that at no extra expense when you are building a home, and it really is spring water. It is pure, cold, unadulterated spring water. So is all our water, as I explained before. We have an electric water pump, the latest thing, automatic in every particular. It turns itself on and shuts itself off, and gives us high pressure. We wash in the spring water, and give it to the hens, and scrub floors with it, and also drink it. We thought it would be cute to have that extra faucet, so we could impress friends from the city. All these other gadgets are gadgets they can have, too, but none of them can boast special drinking water from a tap in the kitchen sink. It will be fun to see some of them try to tell the difference.

We also had Merle build us a fire hydrant on the second floor. Out here in the country a good many fires might have been stopped if a garden hose had been handy. So we bought a length of real firemen's hose, with a brass nozzle on it, and we had Merle make a glass case in the upper hall. We put a red hatchet in, too. If occasion ever arises, we will break the glass and have at least that much advantage. And if that occasion ever does arise, the fire hose will squirt spring water at no extra charge.

Another gadget is my own invention, and I am extra proud of it. Upstairs on the west side we had a long room, thirty-five by fourteen feet, which was to be divided into two bedrooms. I drew out a picture on a piece of building paper, showing Merle how he could make his partition and at the same time build in the furniture for the rooms. He seemed pleased at the idea, and thought I did a good job on the picture. He said most people who want something special made draw a

‡200‡

picture that looks like everything but what they want, and then they get mad at the carpenters.

What he built was a row of various pieces—a full clothes closet, a bureau, a cupboard and set of drawers, and a bookcase. Then, in the other room backing up against this first row, was the same identical thing. So the bookcase is behind the closet, and the bureau is behind the cupboard, and both sides are alike. My wife complained that it was taking too long to build this master-mind invention of mine, and that the cost was likely to make the war debt envious. So we figured out that we got the whole thing, including the partition between the rooms, for what two bureaus would cost us, and she subsided. What it does, chiefly, is spare the rooms the clutter of having furniture in them. One man came in and saw it, and went right home and tore out a partition and built one like it. He would come in two or three times a day and measure some part of my invention, and then rush home and copy it. He got his done before we finished ours, and then I went down to look at his to see if I was going to like mine. The built-in bureaus have mirrors and electric lights, and the bookcases have adjustable shelves. I think it's a nice gadget, and particularly because it's really the only gadget in the house I can take credit for.

Merle ran a conduit up through the walls so the telephone man could come in without boring holes everywhere, and the telephone man said he was amazed. He also ran conduits for the radio, and didn't seem to think this was as unusual as we thought. He got a pull-down stairway for the attic, and carried the gadget idea so far he convinced us to have aluminum windows and a heatolator. Even a tell-tale light on the cellar circuit can be construed as a gadget in these parts, and a houseful of such things, which had hitherto escaped us as adjuncts of modern living, give us the feeling that "an old fort" hardly describes our commodious, comfortable, and convenient dwelling.

When you think things through, some of these gadgets make sense, even if they threaten to spoil us and sap from us all vestige of those antique Yankee qualities so much admired. The door chimes, for instance, will undoubtedly prove a boon when we are regulated completely to a gadgeted life. Because nobody ever stands at the kitchen sink to look out on the back steps, the way Great-grandmother did in her dishpan days. A stranger could get as far as the push-button and nobody the wiser. Because we have a dishwashing machine now.

WHEN our big house burned, we lost, also, a summer kitchen, and the new house has one just as good. A lot of people have inquired why we felt the need of a summer kitchen when our regular kitchen is big enough to hold dances in, and I have evaded an honest reply.

That is because my honest reply would startle them, and they wouldn't believe it, and I would have to go into details. We have a summer kitchen because I like strawberry shortcake, and it is a long story without any great moral or any particular message to the world at large. Building the house myself, I wanted a place to celebrate the Fourth of July, and by combining Independence Day and Strawberry Shortcake you have the reason why our new house has a summer kitchen we don't really need.

It was the year Jack Dempsey poked Georges Carpentier, and I imagine I remember it better than they do. It was 1919, and I was a little boy in school in another town. My Aunt Lillian chose the Fourth of July

‡203‡

that year to pay one of her inspection visits to Grandfather, and she arrived that morning by train to pick me up for the excursion.

It was hot that day—a blistering quiet heat without a breath of wind to assuage the sweat. We arrived at the Falls on the trolley car exhausted and damp, for with every window open that trolley car never went fast enough on a hot Fourth of July to take care of even the motorman. Of course, this wasn't one of your city trolleys. This line ran off across country with hourly service each way, and was more of an electric railway than a commuter's convenience. Automobiles drove it out of business a few years later, but in 1919 it was the best way for anybody to come to our town. Aunt Lillian and I went over to the livery stable behind the Maine Central House and engaged a man to drive us up here to the farm.

I feel sorry for folks who think the taxi has always been with us. We suffered that day—a wicked, inhuman suffering that came only to people who hired a livery stable man to drive them up onto our Ridge on a hot Fourth of July. At first the man wanted to say no. It was too hot. The boys were setting off firecrackers, and the horses were all up in their mangers curling their lips. But the occasion lives in my memory so notably every torture was joy. I am glad I once rode behind the livery stable man, even if I am never likely to again.

But it did make a difference when the man found out where we wanted to go. "Are you Lil?" he asked, and my tidy Aunt Lillian admitted that she was. I had never heard her called anything but Lillian—it was respect, deference and love. None of the family ever minimized her name. But she was among home-folks now, and it was too hot to be formal. Lil she was knowed as, and it was because she was Lil that she got a ride. It cost fifty cents, and the drive was a mite short of three miles. I was too young to notice it then, but I have since found that the fifty-cent fare for Lils is usually a dollar and a half for Lillians. It is a distinction founded not on the monetary exchange, but on the personality and character. Away from here, the rule breaks down and doesn't prevail, but no matter to what distinguished heights our family has pretended or attained, the standing in this community depends on things the rest of the world wouldn't know about. And that is right. It is also right that Aunt Lillian should remain Aunt Lillian at all other times, as she so happily has.

Anyway, it was a fringed carriage once, with the fringe and the shine mostly gone. They chose buggies in those days as carefully as we pick machinery today, and it was smart to let the livery man pick out the one to go in. Insisting on a bright-varnished hack was sheer pretense, because the old rough and ready carriages had been used the most. The ones most used were naturally the best roaders, which isn't difficult to see through. A man courting his girl might want to put on the dog, but anybody going some place special would think more about bouncing and swaying.

We came the lower road, which was dusty and deep sand. No paved roads in those days. The man's suspenders reeking across his wet shirt were not lovely to look at, and I imagine Aunt Lillian would have disliked the sight anywhere but in the home town. Maybe she disliked it here, but at least she would expect it here. And we got up to the old house fairly early in the morning without the run-away the man had promised "if some fool kid heaves a salute at us."

It hadn't occurred to us that Grandfather would be

away. Grandfather was always home unless he was out trading, and he wouldn't be trading on the Fourth of July. As we drove into the yard and the horse clacked on the hard-packed clay, we expected Grandfather to come out and see what had come. But he didn't. The back door stood open with a Brahma rooster settled on the threshold, and we drove him away before we went in and called.

"He's gone out visiting," Aunt Lillian said. But the buggy was in the carriage shed. "Then he's walked out to a neighbor's," she guessed. Then we found the team was gone from the stable, but not the cart or the wagon, and we knew he must be up in one of the fields working. We found him cultivating tomatoes, staggering up and down the long dry rows behind the team, doing two rows at a time and yelling in his usual healthy way.

Nobody was ever so glad to see anybody as he was to see us. "By fire!" he said, "I was wishing and praying for some excuse to stop working!" I had a silly notion at the time that the Fourth of July constituted more or less of a holiday, but later I found that cultivating tomatoes needs doing when it needs to be done, and that nothing short of Sunday should deter a faithful husbandman. Grandfather unhitched the cultivator and left it in the rows. He divided the team and slapped them with his hat, which made them head for the barn unassisted. And the three of us pulled over into the shade of an ash tree and sat on the grass to talk.

"Oh, Lil," Grandfather said, "I'm so glad to see you. I been having a lonesome spell, and it hasn't done me a bit of good." He talked on and on, more than I ever heard him talk before or after, and spent all the rest of that day recalling things out of his own life—a sad kind of a recital for the days that were gone.

Then he jumped up and said, "I'm hungry!" Aunt Lillian said, "Oh, Father—it's so hot!" She smiled somewhat bravely, with an air of, 'I'll cook something if you'll eat it, but I hate the thought." Grandfather, of course, was equal any time to a real meal, and the heat of the day didn't strike him as any excuse for holding back. I remember I felt more like Aunt Lillian than I did like Grandfather.

But that was destined to be a real day, and Grandfather had a role to play in something stronger than ordinary appetite would dictate. We went down into the spring field and picked our three straw hats full of strawberries. Not wild ones, but the big ones Grandfather grew. Then I carried two hats, and Grandfather filled his hands against his chest with some more. Aunt Lillian filled her hand, too, and we walked in the shimmering heat up to the house and found the rooster back on the door sill. Aunt Lillian said something about him, and Grandfather said, "He's company."

Then Aunt Lillian made a strawberry shortcake. I never knew she could cook. I just hadn't happened to see her cook, and at that time I probably didn't know the practice was common. But she waded in like a veteran and surprised me. She tossed the flour around, and got out the breadboard, and stoked up the big stove, and in less time than you'll believe she had a whole acre of shortcake laid out on a platter, and was dumping a gallon or more of sweet crushed strawberries over it and piling them up on top.

Aunt Lillian has lived a useful and laudable life. Her accomplishments are many, her thoughtful and dutiful charities are numerous, her kindness is legend, and I know of nobody who has reason to speak ill of her. If I were to criticize her at all, it would be that she spent altogether too much time doing other things, and wasted her talent for strawberry shortcakes. It is the only one she ever made for me. It is true that one of them was enough to endear her forever to my heart, so I won't mention it further. That one was the finest, most magnificent, perfectest edible ever concocted. The three of us sat there and ate it. We ate all of it. We ate leisurely and happily. Probably no other people have ever eaten the same cubic measure of food at one sitting. It was huge, tremendous, and good.

Grandfather said to put the dishes on the shelf and he'd wash them next week, but Aunt Lillian and I washed the dishes. Then we went into the parlor and sat down. It wasn't so hot in that room, where the shades had been down, but I fell asleep sitting up as Grandfather and Aunt Lillian talked about the family. I woke up and looked through the stereoscope, and saw all my aunts and uncles in the album. I listened to the shells, and read the Lord's Prayer on the sampler Grandmother Rebecca made when she was a little girl.

Later Grandfather took us all through the big house. He had a story for everything he showed us—stories about aunts and uncles away back, and what this one said and that one did. He told us stories I was to hear later over and over again, and he told some I never heard repeated. We saw that old loom leaning against the chimney, and I didn't know then what a loom was. He showed us the hole the cat fell through, and spun the big wheels on the spinners. Some of these things I had seen or heard about before, but it was new to have Grandfather in such a talkative mood and so eager to get as much said as possible.

We spent all the rest of the afternoon going through

the house—board by board—and when it grew cooler he hitched up his buggy and drove us back to the Falls. "It's been a wonderful day," he said, "come again!" As the trolley car gathered speed up out of the village we saw him turning his horse for the ride home, and it was several years before I was big enough to go alone to visit him. Never again, really, did he spend so much time chronicling the big house. When I was there with him alone he'd be tired after a day's work, and while I read the Bible to him he'd fall asleep. He'd rouse with a start and say it was bedtime, and that's about all an evening amounted to.

Anyway, that strawberry shortcake, the best one that ever was made since the dawn of creation, or ever will be made as long as strawberries grow, was eaten off the thick pine-plank table in the summer kitchen. And it was easily such a day that nobody, sharing it, would ever want to forget it. It was Fourth of July and easy to remember. And I built a summer kitchen into our new house out of respect to that occasion. And when the next Fourth of July came around after we moved in, I performed strangely. I do not tell people about it. I do not say that I built a summer kitchen for one day in the year. But I did go out that morning and cultivated the tomatoes, and I sat alone under the ash tree, and I came down with a basket of strawberries. And I had me a shortcake as big as the hide of a skinned horse, and I sat there with the present generation and tried to tell them what it was all about, and why we weren't eating in the other room.

The only thing I lacked, that I might have had, was Aunt Lillian, and that was the one year in her whole life that she chose to go on a trip and see what the rest of the world was doing. I am going to get me a Brahma rooster, if anybody has them any longer, and when she gets back I'm going to make her do the honors up right.

Because, you see, modern living has introduced a new touch, and with a freezer we can have Fourth of July any day in the year, and I have laid away just about a gallon against the time she returns.

D OWN in front of the new house is a hole in
the field that makes a fairly decent pond,
and has ice enough on it in winter so the children can
skate. We're too high up the hill for valley advantages,
and it is only because Great-grandfather made his own
bricks that we have this pond. The hole was left when
he dug out clay and burned bricks for his chimney, but
as years passed it slowly filled in, until it was hardly
more than a wet place.

While we had the bulldozer up here to rout out
our cellar, we had the man push that old pond out a-new
—which means that our new house starts fresh with a
pond near by too. The local fire chief points out that
the pond is a nice thing to have in case of, and he came
up one Sunday afternoon and looked it over approv-
ingly. That may be, but we hope not, but if this new
pond of ours contributes half as much to living in the
new house as that old pond did to living in the old one,
the expense is a minor consequence, and utility is beside
the point.

Being at the foot of the front field, the pond was visible not only from our kitchen window at a distance, but from a neighbor's window close by—which is how Mrs. Mayberry was once found on her kitchen floor in a faint and a pool of blood, and woke up dazed to announce that Grandfather did it, and thus had Mr. Mayberry out gunning for poor Grandfather, who had gone to Lewiston with some potatoes and convinced Mr. Mayberry he had run away to avoid the consequences of a dastardly act.

Mrs. Mayberry, that morning, was doing up her kitchen work in her usual fashion, singing hymns at the top of her lungs because she was deaf and thought everybody else was. One morning she stood at her sink singing and washing dishes for a half hour, and folks up at our place could hear her cat bawling. We couldn't hear her singing, because the wind was wrong, but we could hear the cat. The cat was having a tough time of it. After a half-hour or so the cat stopped. The reason was that Mrs. Mayberry was standing there singing, and stepping on the cat's tail, and she couldn't hear the cat yowling, and probably thought it was herself when she did, and the cat spit and sizzled around and clawed scratches on the floor all the time she was doing dishes.

Well, this morning she was doing dishes and singing, but she never caught the cat again, and she was watching out the window to see the children playing on the pond. It was a lovely morning, and while she watched she saw Grandfather come out of the barn with the horse and get ready to go off somewhere in the pung. He hitched the horse to the ring in the shed wall, pushed around the pung, and then some devilish whim struck him and he thought up a gay and adventurous stunt. He stood the shafts of the pung back against the dash, gave the thing a push, and jumped onto the seat, heading himself down over the hill for a coast.

Mrs. Mayberry was amazed at this juvenile display on the part of a sedate old man, and stopped her singing to gaze. My idea is that Grandfather had often wanted to do that very thing, but had been forbidden such antics as a boy, not out of regard for his own bones, but because pungs didn't grow on trees. The hill had always been there, and was just the hill for it. The pond served to attract attention to the possibility, because there were always children down on the ice and their joyous whoops were an invitation to join in. Anyway, his sudden submission to a pent-up impulse struck Mrs. Mayberry as a bit too dangerous at his years to be strictly fun, and as the pung gathered speed and came down the hill she could see, but couldn't hear, that Grandfather let out a war-whoop, and was actually standing up in the pung like a circus rider. The children looked up, and scattered. The pung whistled down across the field, struck the ice, and blistered out onto the pond on one runner. Then the pung swung, began to turn, and was revolving like a squirrel cage by the time it got half-way across the ice. Mrs. Mayberry had to lean forward and look around her begonia to see what happened next.

What happened was that Grandfather's conveyance struck the yonder margin with all four sides of the pung at once, up-ended and hove him all standing into the snowbank. At that point Mrs. Mayberry fainted, and in falling clipped her widow's peak on the pump handle and laid open a gash. Her husband found her and upon reviving her was told that Grandfather did it.

Grandfather, meantime, had climbed out of the snowbank in good spirits, had fooled with the children a few minutes, and then had gone up to get his horse and hitch in for the trip to town. By the time Mr. and Mrs. Mayberry had got together, he was well on his way, and consequently not at home when Mr. Mayberry came storming up to confront him with a charge of assault and battery. Before Grandfather got home Mrs. Mayberry had recovered enough to give a more lucid account, and while her husband refused at first to believe their dignified neighbor had done any such a thing, he half-believed it after being shown the pung tracks in the snow.

When Uncle Timothy was a small boy he made use of the pond by catching muskrats in it. Once, right after it froze over, he was on the ice and could see through it, and he saw a muskrat swimming around. The air space directly under the ice gave the muskrat something to keep his nose in, and he was going back and forth across the pond about his business, and didn't seem to care about little Timothy chasing around over him.

Timothy came up to the house and fetched the old Queen's Arm, which was the gun Great-uncle Jedeniah had brought back from Wolfe's attack on Quebec. Tim found the muskrat swimming back, and he put the muzzle of the gun down and pulled the trigger. There was never any evidence that the muskrat was offended at this liberty, and probably he never knew anything out of the ordinary happened. An inch of ice on a pond is a physical force not easily assailed, and the Queen's Arm wasn't equal to it, although it had sent balls across the St. Lawrence River easily enough and had made heads duck on the towers of the citadel.

But the force of the discharge, and the concussion of the ball on the ice had lifted Uncle Timothy, lad as he was, right up in the air about seven feet, and had gone off and left him to get down as best he could. On such short notice, the only way that came to him was to drop like a bag of meal, and he hit the ice with the smoking end of the musket pointed down and his shoulder still cuddling it. Then he slid down the musket, observing the location of the hammer and sights as he went, thumped on the ice so the stars all came out and danced, and just as he thought he was all through for this time the musket came down on top of him and thumped him back of one ear. When he came to he was on the couch in the kitchen, and people were running around with hot rags, ammonia, balm of gilead salve, and concerned expressions. When they asked him what happened and he said he shot a muskrat, a number of those present seemed inclined to disbelieve him on account of the lateness of the season.

The exact details don't amount to much, and the extent of Uncle Tim's injuries hardly makes for humor, particularly the broken collar-bone, but as the years ran along this muskrat shooting became a time-honored story, and Uncle Timothy himself told it until it became a classic. Children who sat on his knees and heard it laughed until he had to hold them on, and he would build the narration up into a bedtime yarn good enough for all of us. The moral that he pointed so often and so well was simply this: Never shoot a muskrat, because the bullet hole will spoil the pelt for top prices.

Probably the best story about our little brick pond was the one about shoeing the goat, and Uncle Timothy proved he could dish it out as well as take it. This goat was a billy of rugged capabilities, and his only good feature was that you could smell him before he could sneak up on you. Lacking anybody to butt, he would pound his head against the side of the barn all morning, and come away with a pleased and satisfied expression. His nasty disposition was said to have developed because people plagued him. To plague a goat, you hold a bushel basket by one handle and shake it at him. He gets awful mad. He takes aim, puts his head down, and comes at you with all four feet off the ground. What you do is step to one side and slip the basket on over his head, after which he tears around the world two or three times trying to get the basket off, usually backing up into everything on the farm. In the course of a billy-goat's lifetime there is usually some low-minded person handy who does this to him, and it is known as plaguing him. No matter how much you tell the children not to plague the animals, sooner or later some hired man is going to slip a basket on over a goat and make them wonder. Watching a billy goat get out of a basket is supposed to be hilarious.

In any event, it does make them eager to avenge the insult. Goats are not noted for avenging themselves on the original party of the first part, but will go to great lengths to find some innocent bystander who happens to be bystanding innocently with a southern exposure. This billy goat had therefore connected with everybody in miles, and hadn't a friend in the world.

So the little children down on the pond skating came to this goat's attention, and he went down with his usual ire to see if he could join with them and maybe make a nuisance of himself. He skedaddled out onto the ice with his head down, intending to pick the children off one at a time, and found he had about the same function as Grandfather's pung. He couldn't stand up, he couldn't stop, and he whanged up against the other side of the pond on his haunches with a defeated blat. The children thought this was wonderful, all of them having reason to feel so, and they skated over to the goat and waved sticks at him, and called him a number of names no goat relishes, and inside of a minute they had that goat in a frenzy. He slipped and slewed all over the pond, and the children were not only able to keep out of his way as they skated nimbly around him, but were able to do things to him they had never dared to do on dry land. The goat, on succeeding days, wore himself out trying to butt the children on the pond, and it got so the children skated at their play and paid no attention to him.

Uncle Timothy had watched this from up by the house, and felt the situation had developed in such a way it was not his business to interfere. He didn't like the goat anyway, and beyond resolving to shut him up in a pen sometime, if he could catch him in one, he let it go. Then one day a bunch of bigger boys moved onto the pond. They had come up from the lower end of the road, and didn't rightfully belong here, and they crowded the younger children off the ice and sent some of them home crying. Uncle Timothy was immediately indignant.

So the next morning he put the goat in the back of the pung, and carried him over to Carter's Corner to Coombs's blacksmith shop. Bert Coombs still runs the shop, although blacksmithing isn't the money-maker it used to be, and whenever we get together we laugh about the time his grandfather shod a goat for Uncle Timothy. It has come to be a story in their family just as it has in ours, and while I grant a Coombs is the only man could ever do such a job, I think Uncle Timothy was the only one who would ever think of having it done.

When Uncle Timothy took the goat in, the current

Coombs had horses tied to every ring in the wall, and some outside with hitching weights. He didn't believe Uncle Tim when he brought in the goat and wanted him shod. Uncle Tim insisted his errand was exactly as stated.

Big Coombs said, "I once knew a man was half as crazy as you, and that's as crazy as I'd want to be."

Uncle Timothy said, "I brought him here, because I don't believe you can do it."

Coombs said, "You are just right, and I hope you tell it all around everywhere you go that I can't do any such a fool thing. Shoe a goat! You better get back up on the Ridge where folks won't notice you so quick."

Uncle Timothy had a good time, back and forth, and he heated and shaped horseshoes for a while to help out, and then they got the goat up in a sling and made a set of shoes for him. The tiny cloven hooves called for the most meticulous fitting, and the two men hammered and worked on the anvil while the horses fretted and whinnied and went unshod. Word got around the Corner about what was going on, and a crowd gathered to see the fun. They had to hammer out a nailrod, and make some tiny little brads to fasten the shoes with, but they finally got the job done—eight shoes on the goat's four feet, sharp as needles. Blacksmith Coombs, who now had the whole story as to why Uncle Tim wanted shoes on a goat, wouldn't take a cent, but made Tim promise to let him know how the thing went.

The next day when the big boys were on the pond, Uncle Tim let the goat out. They saw him coming, and got ready to enjoy the comical spectacle of a goat on ice. But today the goat could handle himself better than they could, and he went from one boy to another with ease and accuracy.

‡218‡

After that the goat seemed to be loose every time any big boys were on the pond, but when only the little children were down there the goat fretted in a stall. Uncle Timothy spent the fall and early winter letting his goat in and out. We used to have a couple of the shoes nailed up on the shed wall—they weren't much larger than a dime, yet were hammered out with the same tools Coombs used on his ox-shoes and horse-shoes.

So far the pond has seemed to be the prompter of events slap-stick and banana-peelish—but the way these tales came along to us in our family made them important chronicles. The pond, in my time, had filled in from the fields above, and had grown up to rushes and cat-tails. If anybody bothered to mow it before the fall rains, we got a chance to skate. If not, the weeds stuck through the ice and spoiled it. But the place was ideal for the spring peepers, and every year in late April we get the tidings of spring from that direction. Every lad who ever grew up on this farm has come up from that pond with a peeper cupped in his hands, and has had to have a bottle covered with gauze to keep his prize in. You can put a bottle like that in your room, and all night the peeper will peep, but after a couple of days you have to let him go again, because he has a business appointment down in the pond, and if he isn't there on the third day after he begins to peep, bankruptcy will set in and he will have to take the poor debtor's oath. Grandmother told me that, and I believe it. She also told me that the spring peeper is called a *hyla crucifer,* and if you look smart you'll see a cross on his back, which means crucifer, and it is because he always peeps right after Easter, or right around Easter, and what with the cross on his back he shouldn't be kept cooped up in a bottle.

Anyway, this pond is a long-time part of our home-life here, and I hope in years to come it means as much to others as it has to those before. At least we felt building a new house called for digging out the old pond again, so we can explain about that one off-color brick in the fireplace.

GRANDFATHER made many trips to the cemetery in his time, and at last he came to realize that none of his childhood friends was left to do him the honors. It is sad to look about you and see that everybody else is dead. Not in the ordinary sense of sadness at all, because age mellows a farmer's attitude toward greedy Mother Earth, and he has no need for speculation about such things. Grandfather knew that his chances were pretty good, because he had spent those 80-odd years observing closely how the general scheme is rigged. The sadness was a kind of loneliness over the loss of the old crowd, and it produced in Grandfather a desire to speak well of everybody who used to be in it, particularly as they contributed to his own enjoyment of life. As a result, I came to know a good many of the old timers around here, and can speak of them tenderly and with great love, although they all went their respective ways before I was old enough to split wood. All of them came to visit our old home, and they are part of our new one because we don't intend to forget them.

Grandfather's recollective biographies have not all gone uncorroborated, for local tradition has now and then given me other stories. I know that our fine Frank Farrar had his moments, and that he was not above the foibles and frills of the mortal, and that sometimes he went for days at a time without relieving the distressed widows and orphans or opening his heart to the downtrodden. Not that Frank was a sinner, or wicked, or even queer—but that Frank was a normal human being and did about the same things that anybody else would under the same circumstances. Yet, as Grandfather yarned about his beloved Frank Farrar, I got the idea that Frank Farrar was a paragon of virtue, and had filled all his days with goodness. He assumed, like the gods on Olympus, a mighty and impervious nature not to be challenged by mere men. In my younger days I never supposed that Frank was only another old Yankee who lived up the road and looked like plain people.

My father was named for Frank Farrar, and to my boyhood measurements it seemed such a man must rate with Benjamin Franklin, George Washington, Thomas Jefferson, or at least one of the minor prophets. You just didn't have a father named after anything at random. The truth was, I know now, that Frank Farrar was not only Washington and Jefferson, but he was all the prophets and half the apostles to Grandfather. If Frank Farrar had asked him to, Grandfather would have cut off one of his arms, and been glad to do it.

And now that Grandfather is no longer around to propagandize the fabulous Frank Farrar, I find that Frank had a reasonably good life, that he was not solely occupied in charming Grandfather, and that once in a while he did such things as might not cause a minister to break out in loud cheers. I even learn that Grandfather and Frank had a whale of a fight one time over a hound.

Frank was able to support himself somehow, and must have devoted a certain amount of time to the process, but folks around town would give you the idea the only thing he ever did was go fox hunting. This, in the way that he did it, was in itself a life work, and he pursued the sport avidly. He was a specialist, in that he was the best fox hunter who ever lived, and if in the Happy Hunting Ground he has crossed scents with the late John Peele, you may assume that John Peele has sold his hounds and horses, and has taken up the business of pegging shoes. Frank was easily a fox hunter who, if some shameless hound had bayed during the procession, would have leaped in his winding sheet from his own casket and gone running after with a great enthusiasm and thus astonished the mourners. Frank would rather hunt than eat, but he saw no need of making such a choice, and so carried a bountiful lunch with him in a half-bushel basket, and while the dog circled the fox into range he would lay his banquet out on a rock and dine heavily, his shotgun looped under one arm and on the safety.

A great many dogs assisted him during his long life in this pursuit, and Frank was guilty of at least one profound observation. He said that God might have done better if He'd made the life of a dog more nearly that of a man, as it is a great inconvenience to be breaking in a new hound every few years, particularly since pelts are prime for such a short portion of the year, and a good part of any dog's life is there-by wasted in the hot months. He advocated about fifty years for a beagle, suggesting that useless dogs like poodles and dustmops be done away with entirely so their span might be more suitably spent on hounds.

Some of Frank's hounds didn't turn out so well, and he traded these off wherever he could, and looked around for something right. He preferred a dog with good tone, one that could cry his wares in a three-mile circle without Frank's thinking he had dropped dead every few minutes. His nose, naturally, had to be good enough so he didn't be fooled by last week's sleuth, and he ought to have eyes enough to keep from running into trees. His legs should be close to the ground, as Frank detested a hound that ran the wind out of a fox and made him hole up. Frank's dog ought to keep the fox thinking this whole affair was a gay lark, and move him playfully around within range of Frank's banquet spread, so that Frank could jump up and draw a bead between a roast pork sandwich and a dill pickle. With the right dog Frank did all right and had a good time.

The best hound Frank ever had was a red one that kept tripping on his own ears and looked most mournful about his clumsiness. As a pup they pinned his ears up so he could lap from a saucer. His name was Oliver W. Gensure, because Frank and Grandfather knew a man up to Lewiston by that name and they didn't like him. This man used to come down to Frank's neighborhood on business, and whenever he was there Frank would come out of his barn and make a great to-do over calling his dog, which made Mr. Gensure mad and greatly amused everybody who knew about it. This hound was without doubt the most likely animal ever to bugle the woods of Maine, and Frank tallied fox after fox that the talented Oliver W. Gensure had chased around.

One morning, on his way fox hunting, Frank drove into our yard, and Grandfather waylaid him with some unexpected business. They left the hound in the shed, and drove off up the road to see what they could do about whatever it was that had come up, and Grandfather's hired man thought this was a fine chance to get out in the open air and see if the dog was as good as reported. This hired man was suitably under-witted, as most of Grandfather's hired men were. It wasn't everybody silly enough to work at those wages, but in those days the community thought of everything, and always provided Grandfather with hired men.

This one had a very good morning, in that Oliver W. Gensure took a scent right away, and went tripping over his ears off on a great circle. He bayed and bugled, and the fox thought it was a lot of fun, and finally they came around where the hired man had thought they would, and the hired man up with Grandfather's muzzle-loader and filled Oliver W. Gensure so full of shot that the poor dog died.

This distressing news was broken to Mr. Farrar upon his return, and Frank indicated he did not approve. Several women over in the Borough said they heard every word he uttered, and were curious as to what some of them meant. The hired man felt his remorse at such a stupid blunder was not given proper deference, and his part was taken by Grandfather who thought that support at this time would probably cause the hired man to become uncommonly loyal. Frank said Grandfather ought to have his head examined for allowing such an unmitigated imbecile to run at large among Christian people.

Grandfather said Frank ought to know better than send a red hound out after red foxes. Frank said he had seen better heads on an eight-penny nail. Grandfather said this was undoubtedly an exaggerated statement, as he didn't believe Frank could tell one end of a nail from the other.

Frank said the hound was worth seven dollars and a half, and by the great horned spoon he was going to collect. Grandfather said all the hounds Frank had ever owned weren't worth fifty cents all together, and the hired man had really done the community a service by dispatching this one.

After that they spoke hard words to one another, and Frank finally went home in a huff. He cut his mare with the whip, and so surprised the poor horse that instead of running up the road she just danced up and down in the driveway and kicked, and Grandfather said they'd better shoot her too before somebody took her for a squirrel, and Frank yelled back that he wouldn't mention any names but he could think of somebody who lived handy who didn't know very much. Of course, that afternoon Frank located a new hound, and the first thing he did with it was come over to show Grandfather, and then he stayed for supper, and by that time Oliver W. Gensure was forgotten.

In somewhat the same way I have found that Grandfather's later recollections of his departed friends were well seasoned with *nil nisi bonum*. In one particular instance Grandfather made a lot of generous remarks about an old crony who used to come and buy livestock. As Grandfather told it, this man was the slightest degree lower than the angels, hardly enough to bother about, and his entire lifetime was devoted to just and upright action. The hitch was that, as a boy, I had seen Grandfather and this man trade, and I remembered just what a job they put up. I was probably around ten.

This man came into the yard with a rack-body cart, one with a tailgate that let down and made a ramp for loading animals. He was the same man I had seen before at the railroad station one day, and for a cattle dealer he seemed to be somewhat ignorant of animals. That day at the depot he was loading hogs into a boxcar, and half the men in town were there helping him boost on them. There was enough hollering to put up a circus tent, and not all of it was the kind a ten year old boy forgets right away. The hogs weren't over anxious to start on this train ride, and they fought against going into the boxcar every inch of the way up the ramp.

Grandfather jumped off his wagon and went over to help. He turned one of the biggest hogs back-to and clapped a pail on her nose, whereupon she tried to back out of the pail, and thus backed herself all a-whooping into the boxcar and banged her tail against the other side with a thump that must have resulted in the subsequent sale of some badly bruised hams. Grandfather said, "Throw the bucket off in my yard on your way home," and climbed back in our wagon and we drove on.

So this same man came into the yard that day and said, "I hear you got a bull."

Grandfather said, "Not for sale."

Usually when Grandfather made a statement of this kind previous to a sale it was intended to entice the buyer into thinking he would be better off to have something not intended to be his. Desire must dawn in the customer. But this time Grandfather meant it, and no amount of conversation by the cattle buyer could draw the trade out. He went away after a while, promising to come back if Grandfather should change his mind. Grandfather watched the man's wagon go down the road, and then he and I went out to the barn and turned the bull loose into the lane and chased him up into the pasture.

A bull always looks twice as big in a pasture as he does in a tie-up, and Grandfather made a practice of selling only those bulls he had loose. The buyer had caught him with his bull tied up, and that was bad. So when the man stopped in again on his way home Grandfather said he'd changed his mind, and the man could have him if he'd pay the price.

Modern business is nothing a Yankee trader would want any part of. In recent years we have seen so many pennies split wide open as industry arrives at its costs that I am almost glad Grandfather wasn't here to see it. I do not know how Grandfather arrived at a price. Nobody knows, and I don't think he really ever arrived. Setting a price on farm produce in his day was more philosophy and courage than anything else. The bull calf he had taken "for service" a year or more earlier had cost him only the bull's time, and I doubt if any rational estimates could be made there. The bull calf had been reared on milk that had no value, vegetables that would otherwise have gone to the hogs, pasture grass that had to be fed down or the land would revert to the forest, and various other debits that wouldn't total to more than fifty or sixty cents. Besides, the manure gained had already done a good job on the strawberries and buckwheat. He had sold the strawberries, but the buckwheat had been plowed under to make a better place for a patch of corn. It wasn't all loss, either, because the bees had made some nice buckwheat honey and Grandfather had traded it around where it would do the most good. My best guess is that the bull now in consideration hadn't cost him a cent, but that already he had put money in the bank over and above his keep. But having mentioned a price, and thus committed him-

‡228‡

self to a purely financial transaction, Grandfather now had to say what the bull would cost.

"I figure ninety-seven dollars."

Not having seen the bull, our buyer had no more notion of the actual value than Grandfather had, but his answer was just what Grandfather naturally expected, and he said, "Guess you figure on keeping him until he dies of old age."

Grandfather said, "You'll take him when you see him."

The buyer then made what must have been one of the earlier efforts to put a Maine farmer on his honor. He said, "I don't want to see him. I'll take him. I'll take your word for it, and if you say he's worth $97 that's all the proof I want."

Grandfather looked up, this method being a little new in his experience, and he said, "No, I'd want you to see him. You better look at him." Grandfather didn't like being put on his honor when it came to a trade, particularly mid-way of the dicker.

It took the two of them a half hour to settle on whether or not this bull was going to be viewed, and then we walked up to the pasture and saw the bull standing on the top of the knoll pawing the ground and snorting and he looked two notches bigger than the Boston boat. The buyer easily misjudged him by two hundred pounds, and gladly agreed to the trade at once.

But after we'd rounded the bull up, and had him back in the barn, he didn't quite come up to the stanchion partition, and by contrast he looked two notches smaller than a jack-rabbit. So the buyer welched on the deal, and said he wouldn't pay a cent over fifty dollars, and asserted in so many words that Grandfather had lied about his size. This was unkind, because Grandfather didn't say anything about the bull's size. He simply said he had a price on him of ninety-seven dollars. Anyone would naturally infer from this price that the bull was enormous, but Grandfather had no responsibility for another's inferences.

All Grandfather said was, "You made me get him down from the pasture, and I figure that obligates you to buy."

I forget how this deal came out. My guess is that Grandfather finally let him go for some such mark as sixty-two dollars and fifty cents, because that was just about the usual outcome. But having been present at this deal first-hand, it was strange in after years to hear Grandfather sit around and tell about the happy times he'd had trading with his old friend, and how the old friend was the salt of the earth, and above reproach. No doubt the effect was to prevent my hearing a good many ripping tales, and if some of these old timers had stayed around a while longer we'd have fuller details from my own experience. At least I know Grandfather soft-pedaled a lot in his later years, respectfully forgetting here and there. He made many a wonderful character out as refined and genteel, and thus presented an erroneous impression of those who used to come to our house to call. Grandfather never knew he would have a grandson writing a book about the old place.

SOME of the folks who have lived around here have been notable neighbors, and one of the best things about country and small town life is the freedom with which people come and go by the back door. Grandfather made his boast that he could walk in any back door in town, and he said the same thing when he phrased it, "The dogs all know me." Our old farmhouse was one of the places almost anybody could walk into without bothering to knock, and I am at least a trifle displeased because our new kitchen door has a lock on it. It wasn't supposed to have a lock, but modern hardware is made with city folks in mind, and I have found that most city people spend about a week out of every month locking and unlocking doors.

Now and then we have somebody come who doesn't rate the walk-in privilege, and these break down into two classes—the ones who don't get out of their automobiles until we call off Gelert, the dog, and those who get out but immediately back up against the house or barn and listen to Gelert's ringing objection to their

‡231‡

presence. A farm dog has a great responsibility, and Gelert takes his with much seriousness and performs with such natural ease that some people would think he is trained. He is not trained—he is just a farm dog who passes on those we know and those we don't. If Gelert knows you, you can walk in the back door even if we are all away, but if he doesn't know you he will commence to bark when you are a half-mile down the road.

I do not know what Gelert would do if a stranger tried to force himself upon us. No stranger has ever tried it, not only with Gelert but with the whole succession of dogs this place has had. It's a fifty-fifty guess— he might tear you limb from limb, because he could do it, and he might not. At least a number of people have declined to experiment and find out, and this has given Gelert confidence.

One day a couple of Uncle Sam's stipend users came here to test my cows for Bang's disease, which was probably very nice of them, and they made the mistake of assuming that my faulty vision could see the halos they sported and could observe the divinity that stuck out all over them. Gelert, who should have done better, missed these distinguishing features too, and he put up a howl that made me call him into the house.

Then these two worthies lighted from the government-owned automobile they had, and started for the barn. At first I thought they were cattle dealers, and I was ready to put fifty dollars on the red heifer, but when they ignored me I made inquiry. Oh, they said, they were testing cows for Bang's disease.

This disease has been something of a problem for a long time, and while it is undoubtedly an insidious ailment among cattle, treatment of it has suffered from unwise official planning. At a time when physicians admitted more or less openly that they didn't know too much about it, various do-gooders were making a big issue over it, and under its health authority each state was fighting the menace with good intentions but with varying techniques, and usually with bad strategy and public relations. Maine was probably doing as poorly as any of them, but I think the state wised up as soon as any and did better. Part of the plan was to tie in with federal experts, a word never used more loosely than here, and send them around to test cattle. At the same time, one of the ways the disease spread, we understood, was from feet-tracks of humans who went from barn to barn. Our Artificial Breeding technicians were already disinfecting their boots between barns, and most of us were clamping down on cattle-buyers who came around. Some of the more careful dairymen forbade visitors in their barns. So it didn't make sense when the federal testers started into my barn without any apologies, and aside from the immunities of the home, I had good reasons for stopping them.

When they said they were going to test my cows, I said, "What makes you think so?"

One of them said, "Oh, we're Federal Men." Much of my time has been spent now, for years, wondering why folks who do federal work feel this distinction is complimentary. I seldom find anybody who respects them, don't know when I've run into a man who admires them, and for the most part folks around here dismiss them as parasites, and wonder why they don't take up some honest work. I pointed out that I didn't want them in my barn. I was ready to explain why if they had asked, but they didn't ask. One of them said, "You don't have anything to say about it, my friend, we are testing dairy cattle, and we're going in."

‡233‡

Instantly I had a feeling that this was the wrong thing to say, particularly the part about my being a friend, and I said, "If you do, I advise you to move rapidly, because right behind you will be a charge of bird-shot, and I intend to arrange this situation just as soon as you touch the door."

One of them said, "If you do a thing like that you'll be mixed up with the best lawyers in the United States Government." I said, "That may be, but I think you'll find lawyers are very poor at picking out bird-shot."

Considerable more was said but aside from its value for elocutionary training I think it was purposeless. I specially liked the part where one of them identified himself by showing me a driver's license, at which I pointed out that my wife had one of those, and therefore I'd let her test my cows. The two drove away after a bit, and I went in and telephoned to our Commissioner of Agriculture, who said it was a "program" and while he had approved it, the matter was not under state jurisdiction. I thought this was important, having memorized the Constitution as a boy in school, and I sat around for several days in a most expectant state, wondering how the thing would turn out.

It turned out when Gelert set up another racket, and sent vibrations to the moon several years ahead of radar, and I found the two government inspectors back in the dooryard. You never saw anybody so polite. They spoke softly, and showed recent coaching in the amenities. It was clear that somebody had rehearsed them in the sacredness of our hearthside, and a great understanding had filled their massive hearts. They had identification material, and they most respectfully requested my permission to enter and conduct a routine examination,

‡ 2 3 4 ‡

previous to which they would be eternally grateful if I would have the dog inclosed in some restricted place.

So, you see, a farm dog reacts to visitors within the letter of the written law, and his judgment is to be relied upon. Gelert will also wag his tail pleasantly at real people and escort them amiably into the house without the slightest noise, and sometimes will thus surprise some member of the family who is momentarily unclad and not exactly expecting company.

There are, I know, people who feel such parading should be done behind locked doors, and the whole formality of ringing and knocking is designed to forewarn. It just doesn't happen to be like that around here, and as long as the dog knows you we feel you have some rights in enjoying with us the comforts and companionship of our home. In rural Maine, the word neighbor is also a verb.

Billy Dunn, the deaf-mute who lived over toward Purinton's Corner, was far and away the most privileged of all the folks who have used our back doors with freedom. Others have come and gone much as he did, but none of them ever fitted so fully into the family life and became, for a time, part of it. Billy was a pathetic little figure, and lived all alone in a silent world. He had a nice home, but nobody with him, and nobody around here ever spoke to him. He couldn't have heard, anyway, but the folks knew him so well that nobody ever turned to him and spoke by mistake.

It was enough to wave at him, and then only when he was looking your way. Billy used to come up to our house every once in a while unannounced, and the dogs of that time never even lifted their eyes to see who it was. He walked up, usually in the winter, and opened the back door to get the broom. No matter who you are if you come to a Maine home in the winter, you must reach in through the door and get the broom and sweep the snow off your feet. The broom will be there, all right, and you will find it if you feel around. Sometimes it's right out on the step waiting for you. So Billy would sweep his feet on the steps, and then bang the broom on the step to knock out the snow, and he'd come into the kitchen just about the time the family was getting breakfast under way.

Nobody said anything. Grandfather would wave his hand and keep on eating. Billy had walked over from his place, a good three miles, and if he'd been able to talk and hear Grandmother would have started right in asking what he wanted to eat. But Billy got no spoken invitation, and the only gesture was to have a couple of the children pull apart to make another place on the side by the stove.

Billy began taking off his clothes, and hung each piece up on the wall. He got down to his indoor clothes, and then backed up against the stove to recapture the feeling and rubbed his hands. At the sink, next, he would scrub himself, and pick the ice from his whiskers, and pat down his few top hairs. Then he would go to the cupboard and get out some dishes, look over the things on the stove, and decide what he'd eat. He would crack eggs in the spider, fry a piece of ham, brown some potatoes, pour out his mug of coffee, and then pull up and eat as if no morsel of food had passed his lips since June.

After he ate he would wash his few dishes at the sink, replace them in the cupboard, and get back into his heavy clothes again. Out in the shed he would pick down the bucksaw from its nail, and then all morning long he would buck wood in the dooryard with steady strokes that slowly ate into the cordwood Grandfather had piled off the sled. At noon some youngster would pluck him by the sleeve and would bite a thumb to show him dinner was ready, and Billy would join the folks at table and devour a meal that would keep three men.

All afternoon he bucked wood again, and at supper he sat once more with the family. After supper he would go to the writing desk in the corner, fish around amongst Grandfather's papers and Grandmother's butter and egg accounts, and would find a bit of paper and a pencil. He would scrawl, "25¢" in big black figures, and Grandfather would go into the other room and come out with that amount.

Billy's wages for his stupendous day's work was always twenty-five cents, and there was much formality in paying it. Everybody knew that the work was worth more, and everybody knew that Billy really came to spend the day among some people, and to get away from his lonely home. Everybody knew that Billy charged twenty-five cents just to assert his independence of mere hospitality. It was a token payment, and had no real bearing on the events of the day. So Grandfather passed him his quarter, and Billy would duck his head gratefully, and then he would put on all his clothes and strike out with his copper-toed boots squeaking on the evening snow, and walk the three miles home to light up his fire and go to bed.

This went on for a great many years. Billy seldom came in the summer, because the summers are not so lonesome, but he would show up three or four times of a winter and would also make similar visits to all the good feeding homes of the neighborhood. Then, one year, he came on Christmas morning.

‡237‡

If he knew what day it was, he didn't betray it when he stepped in and saw the tree in the corner, and the children comparing notes on their stockings. He got out his dishes and fixed himself something to eat. Then he sawed wood all morning, and came in to help eat one of Grandmother Rebecca's all-out Christmas dinners. By that time everybody in the family who was expected had arrived, and everybody felt uneasy about the un-Christmas activity out by the woodpile. Billy was so much a fixture that nobody minded his being there—everybody was glad of it—but it didn't seem right to have him bucking wood as if this were any old day. If he noticed the dinner was better than common, or that extra people sat at table, Billy didn't let on—he ate and went back to the woodpile, and after supper he got out the bit of paper and wrote his "25¢."

Grandfather went into the other room as usual, and when he came out he had a dollar bill instead of the required quarter. He pressed it in Billy's hand with a gesture of this-is-Christmas, and Billy ducked his head and put on his wraps and went out into the night. Everybody was pleased at this, because in those days a dollar was more nearly what a day's work was worth, with a little extra on account of the holiday, and Billy was certainly one to appreciate the gesture.

Of course, what happened was what anybody would expect. The next forenoon the door opened and Billy came in, and he'd walked all the way up here again to bring seventy-five cents change. So Billy is my favorite example of what it means to have back-door privileges.

Even peddlers have such privileges if they merit them, depending mainly on how well they make friends with the dog. Gelert has one fish peddler who stops out in the middle of the road and honks, and although we buy from him once in a while, Gelert has another who whales into the yard, hops out, and walks in to see is anybody home. Many times, when we've been out in the fields or away this fish man will leave a haddock for us, and is careful to put it under a pan so the cat can't sample it if she's in. He has to look through the cupboards to find a pan, and if he locates a doughnut during this search he is glad.

I don't know how Gelert learned the difference, but I know what the difference is. One of them, when asked to clean the fish, said, "I can't clean 'em at that price, lady." No farmer should be expected to gut fish, or even know how. That is a fisherman's trick, and is done deftly with a slatting motion we love to watch. It is outside our trade, and is notable for that reason, as few things are outside a farmer's trade.

But the other fisherman, the one who now comes into our kitchen and sits down, was asked to clean the fish and he said, "Why, certainly, ma'am, it's no trouble at all—do you have a cat?" And he also asked if we liked roe, "They're running to roefish this catch, and some likes it if they know about it, give me a dish and I'll show you." During the war when farmers were eating, every hungry fisherman along the coast headed up here to see if he could trade for some butter. When Gelert let them in, we did as much as we could for them, and we noticed that the peddlers had butter in proportion to their willingness to clean fish. That's just a way of saying that the dogs you know, and the back doors you can walk into, are likely to have some bearing on your welfare. We find it so, and we've hung the key to our new back door up on a nail of the great beam where nobody can reach it without a stool, and I suppose in time everybody will forget where it is.

‡239‡

THE house-warming was right after mud time. Our mucilaginous blue-clay hillside seethes in the spring, and its liquid surface wiggles like a bowl of cornstarch pudding. It makes the foot-scraper on the back doorstep an important part of the construction, and my wife said nobody was going to come into her new house until the dooryard packed down. The foot-scraper is the same one that used to be set into the flat field-stone doorstep before the fire, and my father retrieved it after the blaze and kept it until we'd have a new house. "My bare feet wore that down," he said, pointing at the worn place in the cross-bar. Other bare feet and some cowhide boots helped, of course, but every spring and every wet day since this farm was cleared the woman of the house has greeted the opening of a door with, "Scrape those feet!" But even scraping feet wouldn't keep all the mud out, and the carpenters unfeelingly completed their work just as mud time started. So we delayed the moving-in, and by the time the roads were dried out Walter Garruthers could get down from his place up on

‡240‡

the Rabbit Road to visit us, tell us how he fared the winter, and to give us an expert appraisal of our new home.

I was glad to see Walter. From time forgotten, Walter has been a permanent fixture in these parts, and no laudable effort has gone very far without his attention. He knew all our old families so long ago that he doesn't need to be respectful to anybody, and a discerning providence has given him long and leisurely years that his wisdom and interest could be properly bestowed on a grateful neighborhood. Walter came in without knocking, and said, "I was afraid you might have put the door somewhere I couldn't find it."

He pulled a chair over to the new kitchen range and said, "I see one mistake—you got a stove that ain't got a place for your feet. Stoves you can't h'ist your feet to are pretty, but you can't h'ist your feet to them. What does it burn?"

"Wood."

"That's good. I seen a stove once that had ile to it, and I dumped my pipe in it and I still have spells when I sit up in bed and think I'm still running. Ought to be a law against ile in a stove. Coal's all right if you like it, except it stinks if you don't burn it off, and by the time you've burned it off the good's gone from it, and you got to stoke up again. But wood's all right. This farm has enough to keep you. I helped your grandfather cut beech one winter, and I know. I tried to buy some of what we cut, and old Tom said if he was going to sell wood he'd start on something he didn't like himself so well as beech."

Walt said, "What's that thing there?"

"A dishwashing machine."

"No! Does it work?"

"Beautifully."

"That's good. There's a lot of people going around these days selling things like that, and I always supposed not many of them worked. If somebody has made a thing to wash dishes, and it works, I'd have one if I was running a family. I never knew of anything gave a woman so much cause to bellyache as doing dishes. You'd think, to hear them, that dishes are something the men folks thought up to keep a woman in hot water. My idea always was that women first thought up dishes because that would give them something to promote sympathy on. It went along a good many years before some brainy cuss saw through it and invented a machine. What do you do, press a button?"

"Right there," and my wife pressed the button and made the motor run.

"I see. Well, it's a good thing. The man that made that has took ten thousand complaints out of women's mouths, and I imagine you'll be sorry you ever saw the thing. What are you going to do when you feel tired out, and you got to complain about something, and you can't complain about washing dishes?"

"I suppose there'll be something else," she said.

"Oh, I suppose so. But you kicked the props out from under your best beef when you let that thing come into your kitchen. What you going to do to keep the kids in line—you can't make them do dishes. I used to have to stand up and do dishes ten nights out of every week sometimes, which was worse than a switching, really, and my mother pointed out the experience was a valuable lesson and was doing me a lot of good. You can't very well tell a kid he's been a hellion and ought to have his backside lathered, and just for that he's got to press that button there."

‡242‡

She said, "Walt, you're more right than you know, but times change. Maybe I'll just lather them."

"Oh, you'll lather them enough anyway. Kids don't mind it so much as the up-and-coming child specialists think. I throve on latherings. I been sitting right here in this kitchen, the one used to be here, and seen some good ones handed down. I've seen the kids bellow like a cow was standing on their feet, and five minutes later they forgot all about it. I used to yell until I got out of hearing, and then I'd shut up and find something to amuse me. It gave my mother a certain satisfaction, and made her feel she was doing the right thing about bringing up kids, and it didn't hurt me none. Besides, it made me get it through my thick skull that whatever I'd done was the wrong thing to do, and so I didn't do it again. I don't see no harm to a lathering, and I think a kid expects it. I hope you got two nails drove in the kitchen wall somewhere you can put a switch over." Walt looked around.

"No, we haven't, but we got a woodshed in the ell, and we can take them out there," and she laughed.

" 'Tain't the same thing. You cool off getting there. You got to have a kitchen switch and start swinging it right off. I'd put the nails in right there by that door. You'll find you'll use the switch more, now you've got a dishwasher. A woman has to have exercise."

My wife said, "A modern kitchen like this is supposed to give a woman time for other things besides housekeeping."

Walt said, "That's a good idea, but it don't work. A woman that's worth having around don't want to do anything else except keep house. What's she got a house for? These women who think they got to trot around and peddle their clack are the kind of women don't deserve a nice place like this. I've seen a good many women in my day, and some of them I was sorry I ever met, and the only ones I ever saw had any qualities to touch me was the ones that were good housekeepers. It's all right to go to club once in a while, and everybody ought to have a visit away now and again, but a woman that likes going more than she likes staying is better off gone. If you got a house full of modern inventions to lighten the load of housework, that don't mean you got a right to take up horseback riding or nosing around other people's houses under the pretext of being a social worker. What you ought to do, after you push that button, is have that much more time to spend on housework, and just be that much more of a housekeeper. You won't find a single, solitary thing in all the world that's more important, or pays off so well, as being a full-time housekeeper."

My wife said, "That's pretty old-fashioned dogma, Walt; times have changed."

Walt said, "That ain't so. I don't say that reading a good book can't be part of being a good housekeeper. I can remember my mother getting through in the kitchen so dead-tired she would sit in the corner and pant and snarl and everybody was glad when she unhumped and went to bed. Chances are, if she'd had a dishwashing machine, she'd have wound up the day bright and chipper, and have gone flying off to a dance or something. Maybe not, but a good many modern women with machinery in their houses do. What they ought to do is use their leisure time with their family, and not away from it. Nine-tenths of the trouble with women today is they have a family, and then they find out they don't want one. Every time you press that button and the dishes get hosed down by power, you

‡244‡

want to figure how much time it saves you, and then put that much time on being that much more of a wife and mother. That's not old-fashioned—it's so far ahead of the game nobody can catch up to me. What's that thing there?"

"That's a bin for flour, it pulls out."

"How much does it hold?"

"A little better than a bag."

"It ain't enough. A bin holds less than a barrel ain't enough."

"But flour doesn't come in barrels these days, it comes in bags."

"I don't say it don't, but I still say it ain't enough. No home can afford to face the future with just one bag of flour on tap. It's gone too soon, and then one day you get store bread on the table. A bag, you use it up before you know it. It takes a barrel to keep ahead of yourself. Besides, you got to use a barrel up fast or it'll go musty. That way, you get plenty of yeast bread into the family, and they grow up and amount to something. You can't keep house on a bag of flour to a time. I'd change that, and fix a bin that will hold a barrel. You can buy bags enough to fill it all at once, and you won't run so much risk of making your family think you let them down. There ain't no more sorrowful sight in this world than a dinner table all set up with store bread on it. You got water piped in, I see."

"Hot and cold."

"That's good. And you want to keep a basin by the sink. That's one thing modern homes have got away from. You'll find all kinds of people do their washing in a bathroom, and think a sink can get along without a basin. But it can't. One day the boy will stick his foot on a nail, and if you got a basin by the sink you can whip it down onto the floor before he begins to yell much, but you're going to look funny trying to h'ist his foot into a washbowl. Another time somebody'll come running in and say a dog bit a sheep, and can he have a pan of warm water and a dose of Robert's Reliable Disinfectant, and if you don't have a basin by the sink you'll see the sheep die of gangrene while you're hunting something up. And another thing, if I ever get so hard up I have to be here for a meal, I'll want to wash up by the sink, and no amount of high-brow talk is going to get me into a bathroom just to wash. It's a matter of principle, and any good kitchen sink has to have a basin to it."

"Any particular color of a basin, Walt?"

"That ain't so important, but it wants to be a good-sized one. A fellow coming up from the hayfield don't want to have to draw off another basinful every time he slups. It wants to hold enough for one complete wash."

"I can fix the sink so it holds water, and you could use the sink for a basin."

"That sounds sensible. I think that would work, except you'll find you want a basin all the same—something you can grab up and run with. What's that you're making there?"

"That's going to be a cake."

"You stir it by machine?"

"Sure, haven't you ever seen a mixer?"

"No, but I heard of them. I figure they're a bald-headed kind of thing—the man made them didn't go far enough. You got a motor you ain't using except to splash cakes and screw the juice out of oranges, and the rest of the time it sits around eating up the investment. If that was mine I'd take the case off the motor and fit on a flexible shaft and have a thing to polish silver, shine shoes, peel potatoes, scrub carrots, and even wash the inside of bottles and scour pots with a wire brush. If you got a flexible shaft for that thing, you'd have something fine. You don't have a shelf for knick-knacks."

"No, it's made but we haven't put it up. It's going in that corner."

"That's good—I thought you'd neglected that. You don't need begonias and ivy in the window, though they're nice, but you do ought to have a what-not or something like it—little shelves where you can put bright-colored milk jugs and a moustache cup if you got one. Some kitchens aren't worth a cent except they have a couple of blue teacups off in a corner to show somebody has an artistic sense. Kitchens don't want to be all machine shop and foundry. You got to have a touch, too. Have you got a nice blue pitcher?"

"Yes, I have, it's one just built for this kitchen."

"That's good. I'd give you one if you didn't. And what drawer are you going to keep the cribbage board in?"

"Well, I suppose this one, where we keep the checker board."

"You got a checker board? That was old Tom's game. He wouldn't learn cribbage. Well, I brought you a cribbage board. I always give one to people who build new kitchens, and I don't want ever to come here and find you been using it in the parlor. Cribbage is for kitchens."

Walt unwrapped a package from his pocket and gave her a red oak cribbage board, and then made to go as if he didn't want to wait around for any thank-you.

"Come through the house, Walt, and I'll show you what we've been making this winter."

"No—I don't want to see your house. I can tell it's a nice one from here."

"I want you to see upstairs."

"I don't want to see upstairs. I can set in a kitchen and tell what upstairs is like, any house you set me in. You got a nice house, and I come down to wish you joy in it, and find out if your kitchen puts me in mind of anything. The kitchen's all I want to see."

"Do you like it?"

"I like it fine. A few changes here and there, and you got the perfect kitchen."

"Such as nails for a switch, a barrel of flour, and a wash basin?"

"Right. Other than that, you got a winner. A kitchen is good when it makes people live well, and if you don't have a kitchen like that, you ain't got a house worth stepping into. I think you got it."

Walt started to go again and my wife said, "I wish you'd come and look at the rest of the house."

Walt said, "The privacy of the American home is something I don't butt into, but a kitchen is a public place. I've done my duty by calling on you, and now I'm going home and start another cribbage board."

And Walt went home, and that night we had the official housewarming from all and sundry and we have been living in both the kitchen and the house ever since.

IF a country house is supposed to be something for folks to visit, it should also be something for its own people to return to from wherever they are. Our old house was always like that—and besides Grandfather who returned from the wars, it had a boy who kept coming back all his life from roaming the great states of the West—but never a sea captain. That was unusual around here. Nobody in our family ever thought much of the sea, and possibly they were all farmers because the home maintained was so very good. Grandfather, save for his three years in the war, was never happy away from the place more than a day at a time, and once or twice when he tried to be gone for a few days he would always get up the next morning and come home. Once he made elaborate preparations, and had Dick Tarr come up to feed and milk and do the work, and Grandfather was going to visit one of his sons for a whole week. But he got up the next morning and came home, and Dick was surprised.

Dick said, "I thought you intended staying a spell."

Grandfather said, "Did you give Colty any oats?"

Dick said, "About a pint. Did something go wrong?"

Grandfather said, "She'll kick the barn down. She can't take oats, I don't work her none."

Dick said, "Is everything all right?"

Grandfather said, "Dick, I'm an old fool, but I'd rather be home here alone than anywhere else I know of, and I got up this morning wondering if I'd told you not to grain Colty."

Dick said, "I didn't give her much."

The old house, in later years when Grandfather was here alone, really wasn't much of a thing to come home to. Now and then Grandfather had a housekeeper, and sometimes he got a girl to come in Saturdays. But it was far from the traditional neatness even when he out-did himself. Everybody in the family tried to get him to come and live out his days, but whenever he tried it he got up the next morning and went home. The next best thing was for the family to come and see that he was making out all right, and one by one all the sons and daughters did their best.

Grandfather's brother, Tim, was as faithful as anyone, but their differing natures kept them in a constant battle, which didn't mean anything really, and was nothing but left-handed evidence of brotherly love. Grandfather would let the dishes accumulate in the sink until he got a rainy day and could take time to wash them. Timothy always washed the dishes right after the meal. So they'd fight over it, and Tim would do the dishes while Grandfather went back to hoeing corn. By the time Grandfather was in his 80's and Tim was crowding 70 their spats settled into a pattern, and I'm sure both of them would have been most unhappy in agreement.

One of the funniest things was to hear them squab-

‡ 2 5 0 ‡

ble over milk. Grandfather built up a nice business in beef cattle, back in the days when everybody was claiming Maine couldn't produce beef. The trouble was that farmers were selling worn-out milch cows, and milking-breeds of bulls. Nobody around here ever thought of raising beef creatures—heavy Herefords and such. But Grandfather did, and he made a lot of money at it in the last ten years of his life. He had a half dozen bulls in his barn, and bred anything he could get hold of to them. This produced a quaint and curious collection of mixed-up calves, but at least they ran big, and that was not what every farmer wanted, vexed as they were with the idea that cows were to milk.

Grandfather wasn't deluded. He had cows as big as horses, and when they freshened they'd give enough milk to dampen the bottom of a small pail. They'd suckle a calf all right, but by the time the calf was eating they'd dry off to a whisper. If any of them seemed to have extra milk, Grandfather would milk them out in a swill pail and give the milk to the pigs. The pigs came along only because some one of the cows would always be fresh. Grandfather didn't try to keep one cow milking right through the year. So he gradually got into the habit of keeping a can of evaporated milk in the pantry for his tea, and the farm was loaded with cows that seldom got milked. But butchers called regularly, and Grandfather made money when milkmen were hard up.

Uncle Timothy, now and then, would show up for his inspection visit, "to see how Tom was making it," and Tim was a firm believer in cow's milk as a food. He liked it on his oatmeal, he drank it between meals, he cooked with it, and he also made butter every few days. So when he showed up, and got his other clothes on,

‡ 2 5 1 ‡

he'd start off by saying, "Is there a cow fresh?" Grandfather would say, "Yes, I'll bring up some milk," but Tim would tell him not to bother because Tim knew what that milk would most likely be full of. In the winter, at least. So Tim would get a pail of hot water, and a clean milk pail, and he'd go down in the barn and look the cattle over. He'd find calves running up and down the tie-up, some of them as big as their mothers, and all tackling anything that looked as if it might give milk. Tim would feel all the cows until he found one reasonably promising, and then he'd take her up into the barn floor and tie her away from the calves. He'd wash her down, curry her, and make friends. Sometimes these heathen beef cows would stand on their front legs and wave the hind ones around like windmills when he tried to milk them. He'd rig ropes and bars to stop them, and after a stormy session would come back to the house with his milk. While he was there the cow was grained and groomed, and gave milk. After he left Grandfather would put her back with the calves and she'd dry off over night.

In the summer Timothy would strike out for the pasture and be gone for hours. He'd have a wild chase after a milking cow, and finally would come leading one down to the barn, touching her up with a stick so she'd move ahead, and then thumping her on the nose so she'd slow down. It would look like a little boy taming a locomotive, and the cow that had run wild all summer would be stabled and tethered as long as Timothy was home. When Timothy went, Grandfather headed the cow toward the pasture and yelled, "Hi, hi!" and she reverted to the wilds and he to canned milk.

Uncle Timothy would go through the old house and clean everything up, and after he felt he'd done

‡252‡

his duty he'd go off again about his own business. Then some other member of the family would come home for a look-see, and the years drifted along until Grandfather planted his last gardens, and Uncle Timothy and I came back together to keep the place going.

The old home has always been a place to come back to. My father used to come down on the boat from Boston when he was young to help hay, put in ice, or some other chore which was really an excuse to see how Grandfather fared. Or, probably more so, to get back to the old farm for the sake of coming home. When my father comes to visit us now, he betrays this home-coming desire by sitting in the window and reminding himself of something before my time. Sometimes he spins long yarns about the folks who used to live around here, sometimes they are short ones like, "Used to be a sweet-apple tree down in the corner of that field, on the Jacob place. Old Mattie Laurensen lived there thirty-five years and never tasted one of them. Kids swiped every last one of them."

An uncle sat in our window not long ago, his first visit back to the old farm in years, and fell into a reverie. We stopped talking to him, knowing very well he wasn't listening. After a time he said, "That ridge is all grown up."

He pointed at a ridge off across the valley. "When I was a boy that was open field, and we used to watch Jim Farrar yard out cordwood. Jim had a job yarding wood, and he'd show up by Bard's barn about seven o'clock in the morning and team his steers across that field. Took him forever to get across it. We'd watch him, and along in the middle of the forenoon he'd be over by that knoll, there, and he'd disappear into the woods.

for them. But not one of them has looked by the front door without saying, "And to think you could do all this work and not disturb Aunt Eunice's roses!"

To tell the truth, I wouldn't have disturbed Aunt Eunice's roses if we'd had to live in the log cabin forever.

THE END